Using the Big6™ to Teach and Learn with the Internet

Abby S. Kasowitz

Linworth Publishing, Inc.
Worthington, Ohio

Library of Congress Cataloging-in-Publication Data

Kasowitz, Abby S.
  Using the Big6 to teach and learn with the Internet / Abby S. Kasowitz.
    p. cm.
  Includes bibliographical references.
  ISBN 1-58683-007-4
        1. Internet in education. 2. Teaching—Computer network resources. I. Title: Using the
Big6 to teach and learn with the Internet. II. Title.

  LB1044.87 .K28 2000
  371.33′44678—dc21

                                                                                    00-058283

Published by Linworth Publishing, Inc.
480 East Wilson Bridge Road, Suite L
Worthington, Ohio 43085

This publication *Using the Big6™ to Teach and Learn with the Internet* is based on *Teaching and Learning with the Internet: A Guide to Building Information Literacy Skills* by Abby S. Kasowitz, which was prepared by Syracuse University's ERIC Clearinghouse on Information & Technology under federal contract number ED-99-CO-0005. The content of *Teaching and Learning with the Internet: A Guide to Building Information Literacy Skills* does not necessarily reflect the views or policies of the U.S. Department of Education nor does mention of trade names, commercial products, or organizations imply endorsement by the U.S. government.

ISBN 1-58683-007-4

5 4 3 2

Table of Contents

Acknowledgements

This book is the result of more than three years of work and the support of many colleagues and friends. This was truly a group effort. The original vision for the book was expressed in 1997 by David Lankes, who saw the need for an instructional guide for adults to help K-12 students use the Internet. His creativity guided the project as it evolved into its current form, this book. One goal was to incorporate an information problem-solving model into the text; it became clear early on that the Big6™ Skills, created by Mike Eisenberg and Bob Berkowitz, would work well as the basis for much of the book. I am grateful for Mike Eisenberg's support and guidance in the writing of multiple drafts.

Many of the guidelines and examples included in the book were created with the input of educators, parents, and others. Thanks to Melanie Sprouse and Reuven Werber for submitting lesson plans for inclusion in Chapter 1 and to Michelle Herman for sharing her lesson on immigration for the sample worksheet in Chapter 1. Thank you to Armand Morrison and to members of the ChildrenFirst e-mail discussion group of the National PTA, including Nancy McCombs and Sandy Bricker, who responded to my questionnaire on using the Internet with children. Thank you to Allison Nast for testing the Chapter 2 worksheet and for providing details of her real-life assignment to use as an example. Thank you to Judi Harris and David Neils for in-depth phone interviews that provided extremely helpful information on telementoring. Thanks to Erin Rosenberg and Kathleen Spitzer who read earlier versions of the manuscript (in part or in whole) and provided valuable comments.

I am grateful to the network information specialists of AskERIC—Jennifer Barth, Steven Batovsky, Jim Durr, Chris Komar, John Kosakowski, and Carolyn Sprague—for finding quality resources to include in chapter pathfinders and appendices and to AskERIC Coordinator Pauline Lynch for organizing the effort.

Thank you to all the staff of the Information Institute of Syracuse who contributed in one way or another to this project, especially Sue Wurster, for her careful editing and direction; Eric Plotnick, for his editing and support; and Blythe Bennett, for her general support and helpful ideas.

Finally, a special thank you goes to my husband, Jeffrey Scheer, for his patience and encouragement throughout the whole process.

Dedication

This book is dedicated to the memory of my mother, Ronnie Kasowitz, my role model and information mentor.

About the Author

Abby S. Kasowitz

Abby Kasowitz is a Coordinator of the Virtual Reference Desk (VRD) Project, a project of the U.S. Department of Education, part of the Information Institute of Syracuse (IIS) at Syracuse University. She plans an annual national conference on Internet-based reference service for library and information professionals, researches the digital reference field, and provides resources to help organizations develop digital reference services. She presents on the Virtual Reference Desk Project and digital reference at meetings and conferences nationally. She previously worked for the KidsConnect question/answer and referral service where she developed its volunteer training program, responded to queries of K-12 students, and assisted in daily service operations.

She earned a B.A. in English and American Literature from Brandeis University; an M.S. in Instructional Design, Development and Evaluation; and an M.L.S. from Syracuse University, and is certified as a school library media specialist.

Foreword

I am so pleased to present this work—the first full-length book written on the Big6™ approach by someone other than Bob Berkowitz or myself. That's right—in the 15 years that we have been thinking about, talking about, and writing about the Big6, this is the first, full-length Big6 work by an author other than us. This is a significant development, because it means that more people involved in information literacy instruction are realizing the value of a process-oriented, information problem-solving approach. And, I am pleased that Abby Kasowitz, a former student at the School of Information Studies at Syracuse University and a colleague at the Information Institute of Syracuse, was the one to write it.

I consider Abby's work to be one of the missing links in the Big6 bibliography. This book is an in-depth exploration of learning using the Internet in the context of the curriculum. Moreover, from the very first page, Abby challenges her readers to take up the gauntlet thrown down to all 21st-century teachers—to not only use technology, but to use it in memorable ways. Of course, we are pleased to see that Abby considers the Big6 to be the solution to this problem.

This book is impressive in its perspective, scope, and writing. Abby has created a comprehensive portrait of some of the most pressing issues in K-12 education today, including how to best integrate technology into the curriculum. Abby's approach is unique—it moves behind the idea of the teacher as "the sage on stage" and instead stresses the idea of information mentors, including classroom teachers. It also addresses the need for information literacy instruction outside of the classroom. Information is everywhere, requiring students to be ready to use their information literacy skills in any context.

The Chapters

The key to good teaching is, and always has been, good planning. At no time is this truer than when an instructor is teaching information and technology skills—a lot of thought needs to go into those "natural and spontaneous" learning scenarios. In Chapter 1, Abby addresses the issue of planning for Internet instruction. More important, she stresses the importance of integrated information literacy and technology instruction, within the context of the subject area. These are the three threads essential for student success: subject area curriculum, the Internet, and the Big6.

I urge you to take an especially close look at Worksheet 1. This resource is another in a long line of top-notch Big6 curriculum planning tools. Worksheet 1 allows the instructor to step back and look at the lesson holistically, considering all of the aspects of an integrated curriculum. This is not only a useful tool—it is one that makes sense. I especially like the fact that it asks us to consider what the users already know, and how they will fit the new information into the framework of their current knowledge. This worksheet is a painless way for instructors to begin applying the principles of this book.

Chapter 2 is where *Using the Big6™ to Teach and Learn with the Internet* truly distinguishes itself from its peers. In this chapter, Abby addresses the role of "the information mentor" in learning information literacy skills. This is a key, new role for classroom teachers, teacher-librarians, parents, and others interested in helping students learn. That's because Abby's vision of information literacy instruction moves beyond the classroom and into the library, the home, and peer group situations. For this reason, anyone with whom the student comes into contact can be an information mentor. Chapter 2 helps prepare us for this role—to be an information mentor.

The specific content in Chapter 2 moves from the broad overview to the nitty-gritty. The "Examples of Parent-Child Interactions" help parents with no formal training in information problem-solving to be well on their way toward assisting students with information literacy skills. Abby also addresses issues of information ethics, including online safety and copyright. This chapter underscores the heart of the book—an information mentor guides a student to develop safe, effective information practices. Worksheet 2 reinforces these principles, and gives the mentor and the student a way to record the process and decisions.

But, who says that an information literacy mentor needs to provide help in person? Chapter 3 introduces the idea of "telementoring," or using the Internet as the medium for providing information literacy instruction. This is a tried-and-true approach to delivery of information services—the AskERIC service, the KidsConnect project, and several Ask-an-Expert projects have been providing "virtual mentoring" for several years. Abby draws a firm distinction between AskA services and telementoring services, and thereby refines this area of work. In Abby's model, telementors undertake a significant task, and this chapter helps to prepare them for what lies ahead.

In Chapter 3, Abby carefully lays out the treacherous path that telementors face. There are issues of purpose, clarity, safety, and privacy to be considered, and that is before a single message has been written! Fortunately, the Big6 provides a guide for telementors to organize their thoughts and present information to the student. Abby provides examples and ideas for creating a dialog with a student, and Worksheet 3 reinforces those ideas.

Much of *Using the Big6™ to Teach and Learn with the Internet* prepares information mentors for structuring a student-initiated exchange. Chapter 4 moves away from this model and addresses the subject of proactive information literacy instruction—creating Internet resources that can help students develop their information problem-solving skills. Not only can such a resource assist students, but creating this resource is an interesting activity for an educator—it can quickly point out flaws in one's own approach to information problem-solving.

This chapter nicely complements some of Bob Berkowitz's work on developing Big6 instruction from an instructional design perspective. Abby offers an extremely logical approach to creating resources for any grade level. I can't say enough about Abby's approach—it is thorough, logical, and careful. I am so looking forward to seeing the next generation of Internet resources that will be developed as a result of this chapter. I know they will be excellent.

Well, enough of me—on to Abby Kasowitz and *Using the Big6™ to Teach and Learn with the Internet*. This is one of those books that will be used frequently by any educator committed to instilling information literacy skills in her or his students. Abby has drawn upon all of her background and resources—her experience with AskERIC and the Virtual Reference Desk project, her training in instructional design and library media—to create a major contribution that will help all of us.

Thank you, Abby.

Mike Eisenberg
Seattle, Washington

Introduction

Introduction

Chapter Profile

This book is written to prepare readers to provide instruction, guidance and services to teach K-12 students how to solve information problems using a variety of information tools and resources including the Internet. This introduction describes the challenges involved in learning and teaching in a technology- and information-rich society, and presents the Big6™ information problem-solving process as a vehicle for *information mentors* to help students develop information literacy skills. The information mentor concept is described, and the purpose and the structure of the book is also included.

Understand the importance of information literacy and learn the roles that information mentors can take to help students develop information problem-solving skills.

Before reading this chapter, you should be familiar with basic features and tools of the Internet.

This chapter will prepare you to:
1. Understand the importance of information literacy skills for today's K-12 students.
2. Understand the roles that information mentors can play in helping students develop information literacy skills.
3. Identify the Big6™ Skills model as an information problem-solving model that can help students use all types of information resources and tools, including the Internet.
4. Understand the special role of the library media specialist in fostering students' information literacy skills.

This book is written primarily for educators, parents, educational content developers, subject-matter experts, and all individuals who can help guide K-12 students to information literacy by using available resources and tools. Throughout this book, these individuals are referred to as *information mentors*. This term is introduced to stress the importance of information literacy in today's society and highlight the critical role that adults and even other students can play in cultivating these skills. Information mentors can rely on their own expertise—whether it be teaching, parenting, technology, information provision, or a particular subject area—to guide students through effective information problem-solving in all areas of life.

This book prepares information mentors to achieve the following goal: *to provide instruction, guidance and/or services to teach K-12 students how to use the Internet to solve information problems.* It serves as a guide for information mentors, a set of suggestions, and examples of experiences that utilize the Internet as a tool for learning and for building information literacy skills. While it is not designed as a starters' manual for Internet novices, it does contain pathfinders to resources on topics such as getting started on the Internet, Internet searching, and so on (see Appendices A and B). Certain chapters may be more applicable to different types of information mentors (see "Book Goals and Structure"), while the book as a whole serves as a collection of ideas and guidelines for information mentoring with a focus on Internet use.

The Challenge

Students in primary and secondary schools are living and learning in an information explosion. Information on the Internet, a vehicle for delivering information to students at school (Rakes, 1996) as well as at home, is doubling every 90 days according to Jukes (1997) (Darrow, 1999). Children are faced with the challenge of finding and using the best information resources on and off the Internet in order to achieve academic goals and standards.

Everyone involved in the education of today's children is responsible for preparing these future leaders to be effective users of information. In President Clinton's "Call to Action for American Education in the 21st Century," he explains that students' achievement of "technological literacy" relies heavily on assistance from the adults in their lives:

> Today, technological literacy—computer skills and the ability to use computers and other technology to improve learning, productivity and performance—is a new basic that our students must master… The goal we have presented cannot be set and cannot be achieved unless we all work together. It can be met only with communities, businesses, governments, teachers, parents and students all joining together. (Clinton, 1997, paragraphs 3 and 5)

As President Clinton suggests, the responsibility of fostering technology and information skills goes beyond the classroom and into the home and the indefinable spaces of information technology itself. Those who work, live, and interact with children can take part as *information mentors.*

Technology in Education: Old News

It is important to note that the "information age" is not the first era in which K-12 students are using technology for learning. The use of technology in education is as old as the book, pencil, and chalkboard; and computers as we know them have been used in K-12 classrooms for more than 30 years in one form or another (Kosakowski, 1998). Technology can be defined as any tool or technique that a person employs in order to solve a problem (Gentry, 1995).

Technology for education involves solutions to assist students in learning.

Today's technology tools and resources can help students connect to limitless information sources, communicate with others around the globe, and create a wide variety of original products with multi-media features. The Internet, as a set of resources and tools, provides a rich environment for a multitude of problem-solving situations. But along with the exciting opportunities, the Internet presents new challenges for teaching and learning: many Internet users are overwhelmed by the sheer amount of widely disorganized information, the inconsistent quality of Internet resources, and the risks involved with communicating with strangers, accessing age-inappropriate information, and reusing others' ideas and products in original work.

According to the National Center for Educational Statistics, 89% of public schools in the United States were connected to the Internet in 1998, an increase of 11 percentage points from 1997 (Rowand, 1999). As more and more schools and homes connect to the Internet, there becomes a greater need for guidance and mentoring of K-12 students about this largely disorganized learning environment.

Who's Teaching Whom?

In many situations, K-12 students act as the teachers in helping adults use the Internet. Students are often quick to learn how to use the Internet to find information they are looking for—whether it be school-related or for recreation, and students are generally less fearful when it comes to tinkering with computer hardware and software. Students have been known to show their teachers and parents how to use a search engine, type in a URL, and other handy tips.

While children might be able to show parents and other adults how to use Internet tools and features, adults can help children place Internet use in the context of the larger information problem-solving process. Adults as information mentors can help children see the Internet as a potential set of tools and resources to use in completing school assignments as well as solving everyday problems. In other words, adults can help children decide *when*, *where*, and *why* to use the Internet, and not just teach them *how* to use the Internet. In this way, adults are empowering students to use the Internet responsibly and effectively—a skill that can be translated to problem-solving in all arenas.

The Internet

In basic terms, the Internet is a network of computer networks that communicate with each other using the same language (Lankes, 1996; University of California, Berkeley Library, 1997). From a user's perspective, the Internet represents some of the following features:

- **World Wide Web (the Web):** The Internet environment is capable of presenting information through graphics, text, sound, and video, and links files together through hypertext.
- **E-mail:** A system for sending, receiving, and organizing electronic messages.
- **Telnet:** A protocol that allows one computer to connect to a remote computer.
- **File transfer:** Linking to a computer to exchange data files.
- **Gopher:** A menu-based system for searching and retrieving data on different Internet servers.

This book explores the many facets of the Internet and applies them to instructional situations within the context of an information problem-solving process. Internet use in this context can be categorized according to the following functions: information resource, communications tool, and presentation medium (M. B. Eisenberg personal communication, November 5, 1999).

The Internet and Learning

Much of the discussion regarding the Internet and education has centered around increasing funding for equipment and networking in schools, with little attention paid to *how* and *why* the technology should be used (Johnson & Eisenberg, 1996). In addition, once people are connected to the Internet, there is often an emphasis on *finding* information, instead of on *using* information, as Roblyer (1998) calls "the other half of knowledge" (p. 54). The skills used for finding information—deciding which sources might contain the information, locating the sources, and finding the information within the sources—differ from the skills relied upon for using information—interacting with the information (e.g., reading, taking notes, etc.) and preparing for synthesis of information from various sources.

The key to ensuring that the Internet and other technologies are used to enhance learning most effectively is to place its use in the context of an information problem-solving model as discussed in the following section.

The Solution

Information Problem-Solving and the Internet

According to the American Library Association (1989, p.1), people who are *information literate* must "be able to recognize when information is needed and have the ability to locate, evaluate, and use effectively the needed information... They are people prepared for lifelong learning, because they can always find the information needed for any task or decision at hand." (For a complete discussion of information literacy, see Spitzer, Eisenberg, & Lowe, 1998.)

To achieve information literacy, students must develop information problem-solving skills—the ability to think critically and assess information resources to answer questions. In helping children solve information problems, information mentors can facilitate their use of the Internet to communicate with others, find information, and create Internet-based projects.

The Big6™—A Model of Information Problem-Solving

Several models for teaching information literacy skills have been introduced, many of which stress the importance of process, "that information skills are not isolated incidents, but rather are connected activities that encompass a way of thinking about and using information" (Spitzer, Eisenberg, & Lowe, 1998, p.70).

The Big6 Skills, created by Michael B. Eisenberg and Robert E. Berkowitz (1990), is one such model that represents a systematic approach to information problem-solving. The Big6 consists of six basic steps: (1) Task Definition, (2) Information Seeking Strategies, (3) Location & Access, (4) Use of Information, (5) Synthesis, and (6) Evaluation (Eisenberg & Berkowitz, 1990).

The Big6 Skills is the most popular model for information problem-solving, and has even been adopted as the basis for information and technology skills curricula by many school districts and states, including Utah and Montana (Eisenberg & Berkowitz, 1999). Advantages of using the Big6 model include the following:

The Big6 Skills...

- Can be applied to all situations involving an information-oriented problem, from writing a research paper to making a banana split (Little, 1998)
- Include terminology that is useful for all ages, especially K-12 students (Eisenberg & Berkowitz, 1999)
- Provide a framework for action (Eisenberg & Berkowitz, 1999)
- Are easily integrated into the curriculum (Lowe, 1998)
- Involve students in problem-solving and decision making (Lowe, 1998)
- Are process driven (Eisenberg & Berkowitz, 1998)
- Can increase students' abilities to achieve academically (Eisenberg & Berkowitz, 1998).

For the purposes of this text, the Big6 creates a structure, or a map, that students can use to navigate the Internet. The Big6 tools allow students to achieve academic goals and standards. The Big6 can also guide adults in instructional planning, resource creation and communication with K-12 students.

One way to present the Big6 is as a set of questions:

1. **Task Definition**
   What is the task?
   What types of information do I need?
2. **Information Seeking Strategies**
   What are possible sources?
   Which are the best?
3. **Location & Access**
   Where is each source?
   Where is the information in each source?
4. **Use of Information**
   How can I best use each source (e.g., reading, viewing, and listening)?
   What information in each source is useful?
5. **Synthesis**
   How can I organize all the information?
   How can I present the result?
6. **Evaluation**
   Is the task completed?
   How can I do things better?

Some educators of young elementary and pre-school students choose to present the Big6 as the "Super 3," which is similar to the "Plan, Do, Review" model used in many schools ("So...What About," 1997):

1. **Beginning**—Think about what I'm supposed to do. (Task Definition, Information Seeking Strategies)
2. **Middle**—Do it! (Location & Access, Use of Information, Synthesis)
3. **End**—Think about what I did. (Evaluation)

Regardless of the number or names of steps, the Big6 process helps students learn a crucial set of skills. The overall process is iterative, and steps often occur simultaneously. For instance, evaluation occurs during the information-seeking strategies step as students assess which sources are the best for a given question. Originally used by school library media specialists to teach library and information skills, the Big6 can be used by all types of information mentors who guide children in using information resources and tools.

The Internet and Information Skills

The Internet certainly introduces new concepts and new skills for all who use it. But does it change the ways that children learn information skills? Some believe that new information technologies, such as the Internet, change the very nature of information skills, specifically *information searching* skills. For instance, Clyde (1997) states that computer-based information sources require new knowledge and skills related to using new equipment, systems, and applications as well as searching for and using information. (In other words, information is stored differently in computer-based sources than it is in print-based sources). In addition, Clyde acknowledges new skills that are needed to sift through the massive amount of information available, including "information monitoring, message handling, and information filtering" (p. 49-50).

Pappas (1995) agrees that electronic resources require search skills that differ from those used with print resources, and recommends that library media specialists and teachers use a holistic information-skills model across the curriculum, such as the Big6 and Information Skills Model (Pappas & Tepe, 1994). Models such as these allow students to find and use information in any information-seeking situation.

The Big6 model goes beyond information searching, and illustrates that a basic method for information skills can be applied to any type of information technology, whether the medium is a book, audiotape, e-mail program, Web site, or video. The information resource is incorporated into the larger picture of the information problem-solving process. The acquisition of new skills may be necessary in order to use the new tools, but the information skills are the same: define the task, decide what type of information and information sources are required, locate and access the information, interact with the information, synthesize the information, and evaluate the final product and process.

Computer Skills and the Big6™

It is important to integrate the teaching of computer and Internet skills with general information skills as well as curriculum outcomes (Johnson & Eisenberg, 1996). Computer literacy is a sub-set of information literacy, and must be taught within the larger information problem-solving process (Johnson & Eisenberg, 1996). Specific skills and knowledge related to using technology tools include (p. 16):

- Knowing and using basic computer terminology
- Operating various pieces of hardware and software
- Understanding the basics of computer programming
- Understanding and articulating the relationship and impact of information technology on careers, society, culture and students' own lives.

The National Educational Technology Standards (NETS) Project is developing a set of "Technology Foundation Standards" to describe what students should know about technology and what they should be able to do with it. The standards encompass six main categories: basic operations and concepts; social, ethical and human issues; technology productivity tools; technology communications tools; technology research tools; and technology problem-solving and decision-making tools (International Society for Technology in Education, 1998).

Computer skills, including Internet skills, can be taught in conjunction with the Big6. Table i-1 provides examples for incorporating Internet skills into the Big6 framework based on *Computer Skills for Information Problem-Solving: A Curriculum Based on the Big Six Skills Approach* (Eisenberg, Johnson, & Berkowitz, 1996). (See Eisenberg & Johnson, 1996, for a complete discussion of teaching computer skills in conjunction with the Big6 process.)

Table i-1: Big6™ and Internet Uses and Skills

Big6 Step	Help Students...	Possible Internet Uses
1. Task Definition	■ Understand the assignment or question ■ Narrow or expand the topic ■ Identify the type of information needed	■ Use e-mail and online discussion groups to communicate with teachers regarding assignments ■ Use e-mail and online discussion groups to generate topics and problems and facilitate cooperative activities among groups of students ■ Browse the Web for ideas ■ Use e-mail and the Web to communicate with digital reference services to discuss topic ideas with experts.
2. Information Seeking Strategies	■ Consider widest range of possible sources ■ Identify best possible sources	■ Assess the value of Internet resources (and other information resources) ■ Participate in Internet electronic interest groups, e-mail and online forums to query participants as part of a search of the current literature.
3. Location & Access	■ Understand where to find sources ■ Identify appropriate search terms	■ Locate and use appropriate computer resources and technologies through the Internet (e.g., newsgroups, listservs, WWW sites, gopher, ftp sites, online public access catalogs, commercial databases and online services, and other community, academic and government resources) ■ Use electronic reference materials (e.g., electronic encyclopedias, dictionaries, etc.) available through the Internet ■ Use the Internet to contact experts and help and referral services ■ Conduct self-initiated electronic surveys through e-mail, electronic discussion groups, or newsgroups ■ Search the Internet using available tools (e.g., Yahoo, Lycos, WebCrawler, etc.) and appropriate commands.
4. Use of Information	■ Extract relevant information for research questions ■ Keep track of information sources for citation purposes	■ View, download, decompress and open documents and programs from Internet sites and archives ■ Cut and paste information from the Internet into a personal document ■ Record Internet sources of information and locations of those sources in order to properly cite and credit in footnotes, end notes and bibliographies ■ Print Internet sources in order to read, highlight and take notes.
5. Synthesis	■ Prepare/rehearse final product (paper, presentation, etc.) ■ Organize/clarify ideas and statements	■ Create World Wide Web pages and sites using hypertext markup language (HTML) ■ Use e-mail, ftp and other telecommunications capabilities to share.
6. Evaluation	■ Review success of final product in terms of meeting original task (effectiveness) ■ Review performance of Big6 process (efficiency)	■ Understand and abide by telecomputing etiquette when using e-mail, newsgroups, electronic discussion groups, and other Internet functions ■ Understand and abide by acceptable use policies in relation to use of the Internet and other electronic technologies ■ Use e-mail and online discussion groups to communicate with teachers and others regarding performance on assignments, tasks and information problems.

Adapted from Eisenberg and Berkowitz (1996, p. 97) and Eisenberg, Johnson, and Berkowitz (1996).

Information Mentors: Who, What, Why?

As previously mentioned, information mentors include all individuals who can help guide K-12 students to information literacy using available resources and tools. This book explores ways that information mentors can support K-12 students' information literacy development by helping them use the Internet to solve information problems.

The following list represents a sampling of possible information mentors:

- Classroom teachers
- Special area teachers
- School administrators
- Library media specialists
- Public librarians
- Parents
- Subject experts who serve as telementors and AskA service experts
- Designers of educational content and services for K-12 students
- Other adults who are involved in the education of K-12 students
- Technology teachers
- Other students (normally older students) who have previously mastered information skills and/or subject area skills that other students are required to achieve.[1]

Information mentors provide information skills support to students in a variety of ways both face-to-face and virtually: they can provide instruction (e.g., lessons, units); coach students through their use of information resources and tools; point students to information resources and provide students with factual information; and create original information resources to help students learn a certain skill or subject.

When providing instruction, K-12 educators and others should follow a method of planned instruction to create educational materials and activities (e.g., lesson plans, instructional Web pages). This idea of planned instruction is adopted from the discipline of instructional design, a systematic approach to planning and delivering learner-focused instruction. Chapters 1 and 4 provide a set of questions for information mentors to follow when creating and delivering instruction to K-12 students; the Big6 is discussed in these chapters as a basis for learning objectives and methods for presenting content.

When providing guidance to K-12 students, information mentors can incorporate the Big6 process to support previously identified objectives and to utilize previously designed resources to achieve objectives and academic standards. Chapters 2 and 3 prepare information mentors to help students use the Internet and other information sources through both face-to-face and virtual interactions.

Library Media Specialists: Super Information Mentors

As previously discussed, information mentors include people in a variety of contexts who are concerned with improving students' information literacy skills. The one group of professionals who are inherently responsible for ensuring that "students… are effective users of information" (American Library Association, 1988, p. 1; American Library Association, 1998) are *school library media specialists*. In this way, library media specialists can be referred to as *super information mentors*. According to *Information Power: Building Partnerships for Learning*, library media specialists foster information literacy by providing intellectual and physical

---

1   This book is written primarily for adults but some information can be adapted for use by mentoring students.

access to information; learning experiences that encourage students to become discriminating consumers and skilled creators of information; leadership, collaboration, and assistance to teachers in applying instructional design principles to the use of technology for learning; diverse resources and activities for lifelong learning; and a program that functions as the information center of the school (American Library Association and Association for Educational Communications and Technology, 1998, p. 6-7).

School library media specialists can lead their schools in using the Internet as a way to help students achieve educational goals. In carrying out this role, library media specialists take on what Eisenberg (1996) calls the "Internet Challenge." Library media specialists can meet this challenge within each of their major core functions: provision of information services and information skills instruction.

For instance, in providing information services, library media specialists can (Eisenberg, 1996, p.6):

- Provide space, materials, and equipment to help students and teachers link to Internet resources that meet curriculum needs
- Organize collaborative e-mail projects between students in other geographical locations
- Assist students in locating and retrieving Internet information
- Provide advice to teachers regarding use of information, resources, and technology within the curriculum
- Collaborate with teachers on the design, development, and evaluation of curriculum from an information skills perspective.

In providing information skills instruction, library media specialists can ensure that Internet (and other technology) skills are taught in context with the content area curriculum and with a logical, systematic information skills model (e.g., The Big6). In carrying out these functions, library media specialists are at "center stage as vital, indispensable teachers who can help assure that all their students master the skills needed to thrive in an information rich world" (Johnson & Eisenberg, 1996, p. 16).

Book Goals and Structure

As previously stated, this book prepares information mentors to achieve the following goal: _to provide instruction, guidance and services to teach K-12 students how to use the Internet to solve information problems._ This book guides information mentors in helping students develop information problem-solving skills and highlights the Internet as one specific type of information technology that can be utilized to help students develop these skills. Readers can either use the book as a reference tool—reading individual chapters as applicable—or as a comprehensive text on methods for helping students use the Internet to develop information literacy skills.

This book provides suggestions for adults who guide students in their use of the Internet (e.g., teachers, parents) and also includes tips for people who create educational content on the Internet and share expertise with students through the Internet.

Different types of instruction, guidance, and service are outlined in each chapter (see Table i-2). Some general concepts are presented for information mentors to consider as they reach this goal:

1. Identify individual and group information needs.
2. Apply Internet-based instruction and services to identified academic standards and curriculum goals.
3. Apply an information problem-solving model in planning instruction and service and in guiding students through assignment-completion and research.

The guidelines described in this book are based on the Big6 Skills for information problem-solving and principles of instructional design.

The types of materials and activities that information mentors can provide to K-12 students are outlined in the following table. Each chapter offers a set of guidelines and specific examples to prepare information mentors to teach students how to use the Internet to solve information problems. Readers are expected to have a working knowledge of using the Internet, but appendices are included to provide supplemental resources in areas such as getting started on the Internet, Internet searching, and Web site evaluation.

Table i-2: Information Mentor Roles

Information Mentor Roles	Potential Mentors	Goal	Objectives
Chapter 1: Planning Instruction	■ Classroom and special area teachers ■ Library media specialists ■ Homeschooling parents ■ Administrators ■ Curriculum developers	Plan and deliver lessons, units, projects, and other instructional opportunities that incorporate Internet use within the context of an information problem-solving process.	1. Follow steps of a systematic model for planning instruction. 2. Incorporate Big6 Skills into content area goals and objectives. 3. Incorporate Internet use appropriately into instructional situations using Big6 Skills.
Chapter 2: Coaching	■ Parents ■ Educators ■ Technology coordinators ■ Library media specialists ■ Public librarians ■ Other students	Guide individual K-12 students or classes in their use of the Internet for information problem-solving while maximizing safety, responsibility, and effectiveness.	1. Understand the importance of guiding students in using the Internet at school and at home. 2. Identify areas of the Big6 process where information mentors can help students use the Internet to reach academic goals. 3. Establish guidelines for appropriate and responsible Internet use. 4. Identify issues in using the Internet with K-12 students at school and at home. 5. Guide students in using the Internet within the Big6 process.

Table i-2: Information Mentor Roles (cont.)

Information Mentor Roles	Potential Mentors	Goal	Objectives
Chapter 3: Communicating	■ Subject-matter experts ■ Teachers ■ Librarians ■ Peers	Communicate effectively with students via the Internet to provide guidance in information problem-solving, subject areas, and personal development.	1. Understand advantages of telecommunications activities in K-12 education. 2. Identify different types of instructional opportunities involving communication between students and subject or process experts. 3. Describe differences between AskA services and telementoring programs, including the various roles of experts in AskA services and telementoring programs. 4. Identify issues in communicating with students online. 5. Identify issues in participating in telecommunications activities from a classroom perspective. 6. Promote the Big6 in online communications with students.
Chapter 4: Designing	■ Internet content designers ■ Classroom and special area teachers ■ Library media specialists ■ Other librarians ■ Subject matter experts	Develop and provide content on the Internet for K-12 students that enhances learning and promotes information problem-solving.	1. Understand the importance of incorporating instructional design features and promoting information problem-solving in the design of Internet-based content for K-12 students. 2. Identify different types of Internet resources designed for K-12 students. 3. State types of people who design content on the Internet for K-12 students. 4. Identify instructional design and information problem-solving considerations involved in the design of content on the Internet for K-12 students. 5. Design content for the Internet according to instructional design guidelines and incorporating components of the Big6 information problem-solving model. 6. Identify Big6 features in existing Web sites.

Chapter Summary

- It is critical that students in grades K-12 develop information literacy skills in order to achieve in school, the workplace, and other aspects of everyday life.
- Information mentors are individuals with a variety of expertise who can help guide K-12 students to information literacy using available resources and tools.
- The Internet, as a set of tools and resources at home and in school, is becoming more and more popular, heightening the need for guidance and mentoring.
- Information mentors can help students place Internet use in the larger context of information problem-solving in order to help students think critically and assess resources.
- The Big6 is one model that teaches information problem-solving as a process, can be applied to all information problem-solving situations, and provides a map for students to navigate the Internet and to achieve academic goals and standards.
- Internet and computer skills should be taught in context with curriculum area objectives and the information problem-solving process.
- Information mentors can include people in a variety of capacities. This book is written primarily for individuals who provide instruction, coach students in using information resources and tools, communicate with students via the Internet, and design Internet resources for students.
- Library media specialists are "Super Information Mentors" who lead students and staff in use of the Internet within their functions of providing information services and information skills instruction.

Chapter Pathfinder: Introduction

Topic: Information Problem Solving and the Internet

Internet Resources

Big6.com—Teaching Technology and Information Skills—The Big6 Skills™ Information Problem-Solving Approach to Library and Information Skills Instruction By Michael B. Eisenberg and Robert E. Berkowitz
http://www.big6.com/
This official Big6 Web site outlines the six steps—task definition, information seeking strategies, location & access, use of information, synthesis, and evaluation; and links to Big6 lesson plans, curricula, *The Big6 eNewsletter* and other related resources.

INFOLIT Library Research Goal: Implementation—The Building Blocks of Research: An Overview of Design, Process and Outcomes
http://NuevaSchool.org/~debbie/library/research/il/infolit1.htm
This page, from The Nueva School in California, outlines components of information literacy, student skills and strategies, student outcomes, and curriculum and teaching design. Debbie Abilock presents eight "Building Blocks of Research": Engaging; Defining; Initiating; Locating; Examining, Selecting, Comprehending, and Assessing; Recording, Sorting, Organizing, Interpreting, and Synthesizing; Communicating; and Evaluating.

A Measure of Student Success: Assessing Information Problem-Solving Skills By Jamieson McKenzie, Ed.D. and the Library Media staff of the Oak Harbor (WA) Schools.
http://www.fromnowon.org/oakharbor.html
Outlines the seven-step research cycle designed by McKenzie in 1995. According to this model, the student goes through the following seven steps: planning, gathering, sorting and sifting, synthesizing, evaluating, and reporting. The first six steps are repeated in a cyclical pattern until enough has been accomplished to move on to the seventh step. This Web site also includes a link to the Information Skills Rating Scale.

ERIC Citations

Callison, D. (1998). Schema and problem-solving. *School Library Media Activities Monthly, 14*(9), 43-45. (EJ 565 466). Presents a revised working definition of schema, lists four types of knowledge that individuals have (i.e., identification, elaboration, planning, and execution), and outlines issues in schema theory. The usefulness of schema in problem solving and information problem solving is discussed, and implications for teachers of information literacy are considered.

Eisenberg, M. B. (1998). Big Six tips: Teaching information problem solving. Skill 4 use of information: Where the rubber meets the road. *Emergency Librarian, 25*(4), 43-44. (EJ 565 457). Discusses "Use of Information," the fourth stage in the Big 6 Skills information problem-solving process. The focus is on the first component of this stage, i.e., to engage (read, hear, view) information in a source. Suggests strategies for helping students learn effective use of information skills and addresses recognizing relevance.

Eisenberg, M. B. & Spitzer, K. (1998). The Big6: Not just for kids! Introduction to the Big6: Information problem-solving for upper high school, college-age, and adult students. *Big6 Newsletter, 1*(3), 1, 8-10. (EJ 562 891). Explains the Big6 approach to information problem-solving based on exercises that were developed for college or upper high school students that can be completed during class sessions. Two of the exercises relate to personal information problems, and one relates Big6 skill areas to course assignments.

Eisenberg, M. B. & Johnson, D. (1996). Computer skills for information problem-solving: Learning and teaching technology in context. *ERIC Digest.* Syracuse, NY: ERIC Clearinghouse on Information and Technology. (ED 392 463). *http://www.ed.gov/databases/ERIC_Digests/ed392463.html* Over the past 20 years, library media professionals have worked to move from teaching isolated library skills to teaching integrated information skills. Effective integration of information skills has two requirements: (1) the skills must directly relate to the content area curriculum and to classroom assignments; and (2) the skills themselves need to be tied together in a logical and systematic information process model. Schools seeking to move from isolated computer skills instruction also need to focus on these requirements. Library media specialists, computer teachers, and classroom teachers need to work together to develop units and lessons that will include both computer skills, general information skills, and content-area curriculum outcomes. The "Big Six Skills Approach to Information Problem Solving" is an information literacy curriculum, an information problem-solving process, and a set of skills which provide a strategy for effectively and efficiently meeting information needs. This model is transferable to school, personal, and work applications, as well as all content areas and the full range of grade levels. The Big 6 Skills include: (1) task definition; (2) information seeking strategies; (3) location and access; (4) use of information; (5) synthesis; and (6) evaluation. An addendum is included which presents skills and knowledge related to technology that is not part of the computer and information technology curriculum. Contains 24 references.

Planning Instruction Using the Internet

Planning Instruction Using the Internet

Chapter Profile

This chapter provides background on the Internet as used in instruction, and guidelines for planning instructional opportunities that incorporate the use of the Internet within an information problem-solving approach. These instructional opportunities may include classroom or homeschool lessons, online courses and modules, and other situations that contain the expectation that K-12 students will learn some defined knowledge or skill.

Plan and deliver lessons, units, projects, and other instructional opportunities that incorporate Internet use within the context of an information problem-solving process.

Before reading this chapter, you should have:
1. Basic operating knowledge of the Internet
2. Familiarity with goals and standards of the K-12 curriculum
3. Experience with the learner audience.

This chapter will prepare you to:
1. Follow steps of a systematic model for planning instruction.
2. Incorporate Big6™ Skills into content area goals and objectives.
3. Incorporate Internet use appropriately into instructional situations using Big6 Skills.

Advantages of the Internet as a Learning Tool

The Internet can be an important component in American schools. Many Internet features can be used as information resources and learning tools. With an increasing requirement for network-related skills in the workplace (Rakes, 1996), it has become crucial to teach students how to apply the Internet to information problem-solving in all contexts—today and in the future.

The Internet is being used more and more in K-12 schools to enhance existing classroom and research activities including searching for information on a variety of topics, communicating with other students and subject experts, and creating final projects.

Several advantages of Internet use for instruction include:

■ World Wide Web motivates students of various learning styles (e.g., graphics for visual learners and lower reading abilities, sound for auditory learners)

■ E-mail programs allow communication and collaboration between students and subject experts or students in other areas of the country and the world

■ Provides access to a wide range of information from a variety of sources: universities, professional organizations, businesses, museums, government agencies

■ Presentation of student work on the World Wide Web promotes confidence and a sense of importance that their work will be seen by others

■ Allows for activities that can enhance learning of subject area knowledge as well as information literacy skills

■ Allows educators and instructional resource creators to gather and present information and communicate ideas during pre-instruction activities and instruction

■ Facilitates teachers' roles as "guides in the discovery of new knowledge" rather than "dispensers of information" (Provenzo, 1998, p.15).

To take full advantage of the Internet's educational potentials, its use must be integrated into the instruction of general information skills and content-related objectives (Eisenberg & Johnson, 1996). This kind of integrated curriculum fosters information and technology-use skills that students can apply to real-world information problems. In this way, teaching with the Internet presents great opportunities for collaboration between teachers, library media specialists, and others.

The Internet also introduces many challenges in instruction. Some commonly-recognized issues include Internet safety (protecting students from sharing personal information with strangers), copyright (properly citing Internet resources), inconsistency of resource quality, accuracy and appropriateness, and student and classroom management (e.g., keeping students "on task" despite the distractions resulting from Internet browsing). As the Internet becomes more and more a part of everyday teaching and learning, teachers, library media specialists, and others adopt methods for handling these challenges. For instance, many school districts have created acceptable use policies requiring students and parents to agree to a set of terms before a student is allowed to use the Internet at school. See Chapter 2 for further discussion of these issues as well as some solutions.

Recognizing the Internet's Instructional Limits

Internet resources must be able to support instructional objectives as well as other characteristics and logistics. According to Judi Harris (1998, p. 9), the Internet should only be used in instruction when it is used to either enable students to do something they couldn't do before, or to do something better than they could before.

With all the hype about the wealth of current information available on the Internet, it is tempting to try to work some form of Internet use into a lesson whenever possible. But the Internet should not be used just because it is available. Many times, students are better off searching the library catalog or periodicals database, browsing an encyclopedia or almanac, or calling a local expert on the phone. Classroom teachers should consult with library media specialists during the instructional planning process in order to identify appropriate resources for a given lesson or activity. The end result may or may not include use of the Internet.

Planning Instruction with the Internet

This section explains how integrated lessons can be planned and delivered using a systematic approach to planning instruction. Effective instruction requires a large amount of planning and preparation. This is true for all kinds of instruction, especially situations that incorporate the Internet's massive collection of content and tools. The following questions are based on principles of instructional design—a systematic approach to planning and implementing learner-focused instruction. The guidelines presented are adapted from a systems approach model for designing instruction (Dick & Carey, 1996). Big6 Skills are incorporated within this process at the level of _instructional objectives_ (i.e., What will the students learn?). The questions presented below are designed to help teachers, library media specialists, parents, online course developers, and others make decisions in planning and delivering units and lessons that combine content area learning with information problem-solving and Internet skills development. These issues are addressed behind-the-scenes, before instruction takes place.

This guide assumes that those involved in planning instruction have expertise in the content area taught (or access to others with this expertise), have an understanding of the K-12 curriculum and related academic standards, and have expertise in teaching students of a particular age group. Educators in different roles will focus more on answering certain questions than on answering others (e.g., curriculum developers may be involved in a general analysis of the students and in setting general goals, as illustrated in the first question and part of the second question).

It is also assumed that the Big6 has been introduced previously to the students and that they have some level of proficiency with the steps. If the Big6 process is new to the students, information mentors can present the process and steps in the context of a curriculum-related or other relevant activity.

Planning Instruction at a Glance

1. **Assess Learners**—Who are the learners?
2. **Determine Goals**—What should the students know?
3. **Create Objectives**—How will students achieve these goals and demonstrate what they've learned?
4. **Plan Activities and Select Media**—How can I plan a lesson using the Internet that will help the students achieve the objectives?
5. **Organize Materials and Resources**—How will I prepare to carry out the lesson?
6. **Set Agenda**—How will I carry out my plan?
7. **Evaluate Instruction**—How can I improve next time?

1. **Assess Learners:** *Who are the learners?*

Some teachers spend each day with the same group of students, but different questions should be asked in different situations. When considering Internet use, for instance:

- **What do the students know about the subject?**

  What have the students covered in previous grades? What have they achieved up to this point?

- **How much/what kinds of Internet experience have the students had?**

  Experiences will vary from student to student depending on who has Internet access at home, or whose parents are active Internet users. Instruction should accommodate students at all levels.

- **What do the students know about information problem-solving?**

  Have the students learned the steps of the Big6? Do the students demonstrate an understanding of the process as a whole?

2. **Determine Goals:** *What should the students know?*

Regardless of the subject or topic, there should be some level of skill or knowledge that indicates successful completion of the particular lesson.

The first level of the goal-setting process involves making a general statement about what students should know or be able to achieve. This is sometimes called the educational goal:

> *Examples: Educational Goals*
>
> According to National Geography Standards, upper elementary students should "know the location of places, geographic features, and patterns of the environment" (McREL, 1997).
>
> According to the grade 4 science curriculum at a Central New York elementary school, students must develop problem-solving skills including defining the problem, obtaining data, organizing data, analyzing data, and decision making (Fayetteville-Manlius Schools, 1996).

Based on learner characteristics and educational goals as defined by curriculum and standards, a statement can be made connecting what students currently know to what they should know. This is defined as the *need* (Dick & Carey, 1996), or gap in knowledge or skill. The need provides a reason for a particular lesson and helps guide the entire instructional process. For many teachers, this need may be rigidly guided by school curriculum for a particular grade level and subject area, but consider this step in order to identify the focus of an instructional situation.

> *Example: Instructional Need*
>
> The third graders at West Street Elementary have had no formal experience researching characteristics of various places and people living outside the local community, but according to National Geography Standards, all upper elementary students should ask and seek to answer questions of this nature.

or

> Half of the students in the third grade at West Street Elementary have a working knowledge of at least one e-mail program, but all of these students must be proficient in using an e-mail program in order to communicate with people living outside the local community and to achieve the related district geography objective.

Finally, based on the need, educators can create goals that are more specific, or *instructional* goals. These instructional goals are written as specific skills that can be achieved through a set of smaller steps, called objectives (see number 3 below).

Examples: Instructional Goals

Each student will create a written report that includes graphs and charts that illustrate the similarities and differences between the U.S. and a country of his or her choice based on e-mail conversations with students from that country.

3. **Create Objectives:** *How will students achieve these goals and demonstrate what they've learned?*
    After the creation of instructional goals, objectives should be written to map out the actions that students must take to achieve the goals. Objectives are most effective when they include the following components: (1) skill or behavior that student must achieve, (2) conditions under which activity will be carried out, and (3) criteria that will be used to measure student performance (Dick & Carey, 1996). Throughout the lesson, students should be evaluated according to the criteria for each objective.
    When planning a lesson that integrates information skills with content, content area objectives should correspond to steps of the information problem-solving process. Some objectives may relate specifically to the content area, while others may relate specifically to the information problem-solving process, depending on which areas are to be emphasized. It is common for the two types of objectives to overlap. In the following examples, Big6 steps are written in parentheses following the statement.

Example: Objectives

The students will:
- Compose an e-mail message to a keypal from another country that includes three questions about living in that country. (Location & Access)
- Upon receiving a reply message, cut and paste sections into a word processing document or print out the message and highlight relevant sections. (Use of Information)
- Write down three things about your keypal's country that are different from your country. (Use of Information/Synthesis)

Some objectives will focus on the ultimate goal (target objectives), while others focus on achieving steps on the way to achieving the ultimate goal (enabling objectives) (Gagne et al, 1992). Enabling goals can include mastering specific Internet-use skills.

Example: Enabling Objectives

The students will:
- When presented with a highlighted text or object on a World Wide Web page, click on the highlighted text or object so that the Web browser moves to a new Web page or part of the current page.
- After composing a message in an e-mail program, send the message by following the appropriate commands in the e-mail program.

In some cases, Internet-related enabling objectives may be included in the computer skills curriculum. Classroom teachers and library media specialists may need to collaborate with technology teachers to ensure that students master these skills so that the students are prepared to perform content-area objectives.

4. **Plan Activities and Select Media:** *How can I plan a lesson using the Internet that will help the students achieve the objectives?*

Based on the objectives, the lesson should be designed to provide information to the students and allow them to find and use information independently. Although the methods and strategies used may depend on the educational philosophies of the school and particular teachers, lessons should accommodate the needs and abilities of a targeted group of students and should consider logistical issues.

For example, a lesson involving use of Web resources can be achieved in a few different ways. To emphasize "Use of Information," you can provide access or direct paths to specific Web sites and pages. Direct paths are helpful when class time is limited and when working with students who require more structure. Direct links also help students avoid wandering to inappropriate Web sites. To emphasize "Location & Access," give students choices of Web sites to visit, or have them conduct their own searches using Internet search engines. (See Sample Lesson Plans and Projects.)

Table 1-1 includes examples of methods for incorporating Internet use into instruction:

Table 1-1: Sample Internet Uses for Instruction

The Internet as...	Sample Use	Advantages	Considerations	Examples/Supporting Resources
Set of Information Resources	The instructor locates suitable Web sites prior to instruction and stores them by: ■ Saving them in a bookmark (or "favorites") file. ■ Including them in a class Web page. ■ Listing them in a student workbook or worksheet.	■ Saves time during instruction. ■ Good way to present selected resources to serve as a "jumping off" point (if emphasis is not on Location & Access). ■ Reduces the possibility of students wandering to unsuitable sites.	■ Carefully evaluate Web sites to which students will be referred. ■ Draw clear connections between resources and lesson goals (e.g., organize list of resources within logical categories).	These sites of lesson plans include lists of Web sites to supplement the lessons: ■ "Black and White in United States History: A Gray Area" (*The New York Times* on the Web) <http://www.nytimes.com/learning/teachers/lessons/981116mon day.html> ■ "Earth Day Every Day" (Microsoft Encarta) <http://encarta.msn.com/alexandria/templates/lessonFull.asp?page=2724>

Table 1-1: Sample Internet Uses for Instruction (cont.)

The Internet as...	Sample Use	Advantages	Considerations	Examples/Supporting Resources
	If the objectives relate to Location & Access skills, the instructor can include time during instruction (or as homework) for students to search for resources. The instructor can suggest search engines and search terms.	■ Helps students develop search techniques. ■ Good way to teach evaluation of research skills.	■ May need to monitor students closely during browsing and searching activities. ■ May need to teach basic searching skills.	See Appendix B for list of resources that teach Internet searching skills.
Communications Technology (See Chapter 3 for tips on communicating with students via the Internet)	Teachers can set up a class mailing list to distribute project information, and foster communication between students.	■ Encourages students to share ideas with each other. ■ Allows students to participate in conversations who may be uncomfortable speaking during class. ■ Allows the teacher to be available for help with projects outside of class.	■ Teacher should set time limits as to when he/she is available to answer student questions. ■ Teacher should enforce "Netiquette" as established by school acceptable use policy.	Resources on "Netiquette": ■ http://www.albion. com/netiquette/ introduction.html (The Core Rules of Netiquette) ■ http://www.dtcc. edu/cs/rfc1855.html (RFC 1855 Netiquette Guidelines, Delaware Tech Computer Services).
	Students can communicate with students in another school anywhere in the world as keypals.	■ Helps students develop communications skills. ■ Good for objectives relating to learning about different cultures.	■ Contact teachers at other schools to establish keypal relationships or activities. ■ Decide if relationship(s)/ activities will be between individual students or classrooms.	Web sites with information on keypals include: ■ Keypals Club International http://www. worldkids.net/clubs /kci/ ■ Mighty Media Keypals Club http://www. mightymedia.com/ keypals/
	Students can submit questions to subject and skill experts via e-mail or the Web.	■ Puts students in direct contact with professionals. ■ One-on-one attention is motivating for students. ■ Experts serve as information resources beyond what is available locally.	■ Teachers should identify, or help students identify, appropriate "AskA" services. ■ Teacher may need to compose messages for younger students. ■ Encourage students to provide feedback to experts after receiving response.	See these sites for tips on using AskA services in the classroom: ■ AskA+ Locator http://www.vrd.org /locator/subject. html for a listing of AskA services for K-12 education ■ VRD Learning Center http://www. vrd.org/k12/ k-12home.html

Table 1-1: Sample Internet Uses for Instruction (cont.)

The Internet as...	Sample Use	Advantages	Considerations	Examples/Supporting Resources
	Students can participate in telementoring relationships for assistance in long-term projects.	■ Allows students to build long-term relationships with mentoring adults. ■ One-on-one attention is motivating for students. ■ Mentor can track student progress and skill development over time.	■ Decide whether students should communicate individually or as a group. ■ Encourage students to check e-mail regularly and provide feedback to telementors. ■ Teachers should have clear goals for student(s) to achieve as a result of participation. ■ Teacher should make initial arrangements with telementoring program.	■ **Electronic Emissary** Texas Center for Educational Technology (TCET) and the University of Texas at Austin's College of Education, http://www.tapr.org/emissary/ ■ **TeleMentoring Young Women in Science, Engineering, & Computing** EDC/Center for Children & Technology, funded by National Science Foundation, http://www.edc.org/CCT/telementoring/ ■ **International Telementor Center** Colorado State University http://www.telementor.org/hp/index.html
Presentation Medium (See Chapter 4 for tips on designing content on the Internet for students).	Instructor can develop a Web page to present information during a lesson including: ■ Lesson objectives and requirements ■ Examples of explanations of concepts ■ Supporting graphics, sound, animation, etc. ■ Links to related resources.	■ Provides resource that students can access during class or outside of class. ■ Can provide links to related information for students to explore on their own. ■ Allows for inclusion of motivating graphics and other features. ■ Easily updated and revised.	■ Instructional Web page can serve the same general purpose as a student worksheet or workbook.	■ See Appendix H for resources on designing Web pages.

Table 1-1: Sample Internet Uses for Instruction (cont.)

The Internet as...	Sample Use	Advantages	Considerations	Examples/Supporting Resources
	Students can create a Web page as final product for a lesson.	■ Allows students to share work with classmates and other Internet users. ■ Application for synthesis skills.	■ Student must have access to a server or create locally on a hard drive. ■ Student should have knowledge of Web page design.	■ See examples of student work on the Web at ThinkQuest (www.thinkquest.org)

5. **Organize Materials and Resources:** *How will I prepare the lesson?*
This step involves the physical preparation required to ensure that the lesson runs smoothly. The level of preparation depends upon the amount of structure required in the classroom. Activities here include saving Web sites in a "bookmark" or "favorite sites" file, contacting classrooms to set up a collaborative e-mail activity, designing a Web page for students to use during instruction (see Chapter 4), and practicing with an HTML-authoring tool that you plan to use during the lesson.
Physical logistics and other issues to consider are:
- Location and accessibility of computers (i.e., will the class need to move to the computer room or library media center during the lesson?)
- Number of computers with Internet access available
- Staff available for instructional support if needed
- Staff available for technical support if needed
- Equipment for presenting information (overhead projector, LCD panel/projector, etc.).

There are special issues to consider when preparing Web-based content for instruction (as opposed to face-to-face instruction with teacher and students). See Chapter 4 for a discussion of these issues.

6. **Set Agenda:** *How will I carry out my plan?*
After the planning is complete, it is time to deliver the instruction. As any teacher knows, things do not always proceed in the classroom as planned. Since many educators are new to teaching with the Internet, it is more important than ever to be flexible during instruction. Be prepared for computers to crash and for students to write e-mail messages to friends or to explore unexpected Web sites during a lesson. Rely on school policies for acceptable use of the Internet (if you don't have an Internet use policy, see that one is written as soon as possible) (see Appendix G, Online Safety). Instruction with the Internet will improve with experience, and each lesson should be viewed as a step toward improvement.

7. **Evaluate Instruction:** *How can I improve next time?*
Evaluation is a major component of educational technology and can occur throughout the entire process. It helps us determine the effectiveness and efficiency of the lesson. Issues to focus on include the following:

- How well did the students achieve the objectives?
- How well did the students carry out the steps of the information problem-solving process in completing the objectives?
- What actions did I take in planning that can be eliminated next time? What actions did I leave out that I should include next time?
- What additional training or practice do I require to be a more efficient Internet user?
- What worked and what didn't work during the delivery of instruction?

One can't possibly keep up with the constant changes in instructional technology and the possibilities for new, exciting learning opportunities without ongoing training and professional development. It is important to take advantage of such opportunities whenever possible.

Sample Lesson Plans and Projects

There are many possibilities for incorporating the Internet into classroom lessons in ways that teach content while promoting an information problem-solving approach. This section presents three sample lesson plans that incorporate the Internet into a subject area lesson using the Big6.

- Elementary School—Living in Italy
- Middle School—How to Buy a Car
- High School—Jerusalem Neighborhoods

Title: Living in Italy[2]

Author: Abby S. Kasowitz
Subject Area: Social Studies—Cultures, Geography
Grade: 2
Big6™ Skills Emphasized:
- Big6 Skill 3—Location & Access
- Big6 Skill 4—Use of Information
- Big6 Skill 5—Synthesis

(Big6 Skills were presented during instruction using the "Super 3.")

Internet Uses:

- Communication—E-mail students in a school in Italy.
- Information resources—Read Web pages with information on Italy.

Goal:

Understand similarities and differences between your own culture and different cultures.

Subject Area Objectives:

1. Describe life in Italy (from students' perspective) by creating a picture book.
2. State similarities and differences between aspects of life in the United States and in Italy.
3. Identify specific country on a world map (geography).

---

2 This lesson can be adapted for the study of any aspect of life that can be compared across two different cultures (e.g., seasons, food, holidays, etc.).

Big6™ Objectives:

1. State Super 3 steps using "beginning, middle, end" terminology.
2. List different sources of information for finding out about Italy (including print and electronic sources). (BEGINNING: Information Seeking Strategies)
3. Determine ways to look for information about Italy in types of sources discussed (e.g., how to find books, Web sites, people, etc.). (MIDDLE: Location & Access)
4. Write a letter to students in Italy containing questions and send the letter via e-mail. (MIDDLE: Location & Access)
5. Find answers to questions in e-mail response from Italian students. (MIDDLE: Use of Information)
6. Create a book about life in Italy with the narrative based on information from the e-mail response and accompanying illustrations. (MIDDLE: Synthesis).

Overview:

This lesson uses the Internet to allow students to learn cultural differences and similarities by contacting students in another country. The objectives and activities can be adapted to lessons involving multi-cultural studies in any context. This particular lesson focuses on specific aspects of life from the perspective of a second grade student. During each activity, the library media specialist and teacher point out the corresponding step in the Super 3 process.

Students work with a teacher and library media specialist to learn some background about living in Italy and then brainstorm specific questions about the topic and some information sources to help the students find answers. The teacher and library media specialist help students compose a message to a class of Italian students at the same grade level. Based upon the responses from the Italian students, the American students create a book about living in Italy by composing original sentences and drawing related illustrations. The students read their completed books aloud to the class.

Activities:

Day 1–Beginning
1. Attention-getting strategies: Show the students a map of the world. Discuss with students the countries they have already learned about in class and point out Italy on the map. Read picture book(s) about living in Italy.
2. Explain project goals: Students will make a book about living in Italy. Students will find answers to their own questions, write the answers, and draw pictures to go along with their written work to create a book.

With the teacher and library media specialist's help, students list the things they'd like to learn about living in Italy and then list sources of information that can help them answer their questions.

Day 2–Middle
1. Discuss ways to find specific resources to answer questions: books (go to "countries" section of library, ask library media specialist); Web sites (search, search terms); people (e-mail, phone, etc.).
2. Help students find information about Italy on the Web and in the library. (The teacher can share previously identified Web sites, books, and other resources.)
3. Assist students by typing questions in an e-mail message for the class in Italy.

Day 3–End

1. Students read e-mail responses from students in Italy and identify answers to their questions.
2. Library media specialist and teacher help students construct sentences and illustrations for book. (Sentences may be hand-written or typed; pictures may be drawn or acquired from software programs or the Web.)
3. Library media specialist and teacher discuss organization of book into three parts: beginning, middle, and end. What information should go first, second, etc.? What should be on the cover (title, authors, and picture)?
4. Students place sentences and pictures on appropriate pages.
5. Students take turns reading books aloud to class.

Logistics:

Equipment: This lesson requires computers with e-mail and Web access. Students may use individual or school e-mail accounts, depending on availability and whether or not students are writing individual or group messages.

Staff: There should be enough teachers available to monitor students' outgoing messages for clarity, spelling, grammar and general appropriateness.

Evaluation:

The teacher and library media specialist ask students the following questions regarding the assignment when completed:

Subject Area
1. List three differences between the way people live in Italy and the way people live in the United States.
2. List three similarities about the way people live in both countries.

Big6™ Skills
1. What sources did we use to find information to our questions? (Web, people, books)
2. How did we communicate with people in Italy? (e-mail)
3. How did we organize our book? (beginning, middle, end)

Instructor Preparation:

Before the lesson, the teacher should organize all of the materials (including maps of the world and of Italy, picture books about Italy, Web pages about Italy, booklet of construction paper for "book"); post a request on an intercultural listserv or make other arrangements to find Italian "keypals" who speak English; and design a Super 3 poster listing the three steps.

Comments:

The synthesis part of this lesson (the book) may be created electronically, especially for older students with more advanced computer and Internet skills. The book may be constructed as a Web page with links to information on different topics (e.g., songs, food, and gifts). Pictures and audio files (e.g., songs) may be downloaded from other sites (with proper credit given).

This lesson is motivating for students, because they receive personal messages from other students their age who are addressing questions of interest to them. Along with responses to their questions, students may receive questions from the Italian students about life in America. This e-mail activity can help students develop their communications skills as well as learn about other cultures.

Title: Help! I Need to Buy a Car

Author: Melanie B. Sprouse
Subject: Mathematics
Grade: Middle Grades (7th and 8th)
Big6™ Skills Emphasized:
- Big6 Skill 4—Use of Information
- Big6 Skill 5—Synthesis

Internet Uses:

- Information Resource—Use Web pages to determine car cost and loan options.
- Presentation—Present findings on Web page (optional).

Goal:

Students will be able to determine the most economical loan option for financing their car.

Subject Area Objectives:

1. Calculate the sales tax amount on a car purchase.
2. Calculate simple interest for the car purchase using the formula: Principal x Time x Rate.
3. Analyze the loan options (percentage rate vs. years) to determine the most economical purchase plan.

Big6™ Objectives:

1. Identify car cost information on a pre-designed Web site. (Use of Information)
2. Present findings in spreadsheet (extra credit). (Synthesis)
3. Present findings in a *PowerPoint* document or Web page. (Synthesis)
4. State corresponding Big6 stage as each objective is completed. (All)

Overview:

To make the students motivated and interested in math, the lesson must contain a real-life connection and must be meaningful. Since students are very interested in their future car purchases, this activity may be used to engage the student. The students investigate the cost of the car of their choice, determine the sale price including tax, and calculate the simple interest of the car loan using the loan options determined by the teacher. During the lesson, students are referred to the "Buy a Car On-Line" Web site and the "Sprouse Bank of America," a page the lesson author created to present predetermined loan options.

Activities:

1. Students are directed to the "Buy a Car On-Line" Web site to choose a car. At this Web site, students can find the cost of the car.
2. Students are asked to determine the cost of the car including sales tax.
3. Students are asked to determine the most economical car loan option offered by the "Sprouse Bank of America" (a Web page created by the teacher that displays loan options with varying interest rates and years). Students must determine the simple interest for the three different loan options using the formula—Principal x Time x Rate.
4. Students analyze the total cost of the car using each loan option and then determine the most economical deal.
5. Optional: Students can create a spreadsheet to show their loan amounts and can use this to analyze their work.
6. Students present their findings to the bank through a Web page or a *PowerPoint* presentation.

Evaluation:

A rubric can be easily developed to determine if the students met the subject area and Big6 objectives. The spreadsheet can be evaluated to see if the students have chosen the most economical loan option.

Instructor Preparation:

In preparation for this problem-solving activity, the teacher set up a Web page for the students to limit the time that students would spend "searching" for their car:
http://forum.swarthmore.edu/workshops/sum98/participants/sprouse/carbuy.html
(The author encourages other teachers to use this page for their students.)

Prior to this lesson, students should practice solving math problems that include calculating tax and simple interest.

Comments:

Students are motivated by this lesson because it relates to real-life experiences and allows students to use the Internet.

Submitted by Melanie Sprouse, Teacher, Lakeview Middle School, Greenville, SC.

Title: Neighborhoods in Jerusalem

Authors: Tzila Yarhi, Miriam Weitman, Ita Munitz, Phylis Goldman, Reuven Werber
Subject Areas: Geography, History
Grade: 9
Big6™ Skills Emphasized:
■ Big6 Skill 1—Task Definition
■ Big6 Skill 2—Information Seeking Strategies
■ Big6 Skill 3—Location & Access
■ Big6 Skill 5—Synthesis

Internet Uses:

- Communication—E-mail teachers for advice and assignment submission.
- Information Resource—Search for and view Web sites with information pertaining to a particular neighborhood.
- Presentation—Upload *PowerPoint* presentation to the school Web site to be viewed with Microsoft *Internet Explorer*.

Goal:

Study the geographical, historical, and demographic development of Jerusalem.

Subject Area Objective:

Research a specific neighborhood in Jerusalem to understand the history, geography, and life of Jerusalem and its residents.

Big6™ Objectives:

1. Understand the assignment. (Task Definition)
2. Formulate relevant research questions. (Information Seeking Strategies)
3. Determine best sources for information gathering. (Information Seeking Strategies)
4. Search for specific information about neighborhoods. (Location & Access)
5. Construct a presentation on the neighborhood using Microsoft *PowerPoint*. (Synthesis)
6. Write a two-page report on one of the problems facing the neighborhood and outline possible solutions. (Synthesis)
7. State the corresponding Big6 stage as each objective is completed. (All)

Overview:

Two 9th grade classes of 31-32 students each are divided into teams of four. Each team chooses a neighborhood in Jerusalem and gathers, sorts, and organizes information. Using Microsoft *PowerPoint*, each team builds a presentation to exhibit at school about its neighborhood. Each team divides into two sub-teams of two students each, writes a report on a problem facing its neighborhood today, and proposes some possible solutions.

This lesson may be adapted to the study of neighborhoods, towns, or cities in any particular geographical location.

Activities:

1. Each team chooses a Jerusalem neighborhood.
2. Each team gathers information on the following points:
    - Neighborhood name
    - Map of the neighborhood
    - Historical timeline of the neighborhood from its founding until the present day
    - Demographic makeup
    - Important buildings and institutions
    - Important personalities
    - Architecture and building styles
    - The neighborhood in art (drawing, photo, poetry, music)
    - Additional points of importance and interest

Each team gathers information using the following recommended resources:
- **Text:** encyclopedias, books, periodicals
- **Digital:** periodical guide, Jerusalem CDs, school library digital catalog
- **Internet sources:** Web pages, Web-based databases
- **Additional:** tours, museums, interviews, correspondence (e-mail and snail mail)

3. Each team synthesizes this information into a 10-20 minute presentation using Microsoft *PowerPoint*. The presentation is shown to the whole school at an assembly. The presentation should contain a cover slide, text, pictures, maps, audio and video clips, and a rich and diverse bibliography.

4. Following the presentation, groups of two (from each team of four) write a report on their chosen neighborhood.

5. Students upload their *PowerPoint* presentations to the school Web site after saving files in HTML format.

Logistics:

Equipment: During the assignment, the teams have access to two labs outfitted with networked computers using frame relay connection (20 machines). In addition to scheduled class time, the labs are open and accessible throughout the school day as long as no other class is using them. In addition, four stations are available in the school library.

Staff: Two information technology teachers work with the teams in classes for two hours a week. One library media specialist works with the classes one hour a week, and two homeroom teachers are also involved in overseeing the project.

Evaluation:

The evaluation process will consist of three aspects:
1. Reflective evaluation
2. Peer evaluation
3. Instructor evaluation

Evaluation instruments are based upon project requirements as outlined above.

Comments:

It is helpful if the instructor creates a Web page with some basic links for starting the project. Extra credit is offered to teams who submit good sites to add to the list.

Submitted by Reuven Werber, Ed-tech coordinator, Neveh Channah Torah High School for Girls, Etzion Bloc, Israel.

Planning Instruction Using the Internet

Worksheet 1

Instructions: This worksheet is intended to help teachers and other information mentors plan, implement and evaluate lessons involving the Internet. This worksheet considers the instructional design approach, the Big6 Skills, and highlights issues to consider when using the Internet in instruction. Decisions can be made in a different order than suggested below, and each step can be addressed more than once. Notes can be made right on the worksheet or on a separate piece of paper or word processing file.

Lesson or Activity Profile

Subject Area:

Unit:

Topic:

Grade Level:

Planning Steps

Planning Instruction at a Glance

1. Assess Learners
2. Determine Goals
3. Create Objectives
4. Plan Activities and Select Media
5. Organize Materials and Resources
6. Set Agenda
7. Evaluate Instruction

---

1. **Assess Learners:** _What do the students currently know?_

    Subject Knowledge or Experience:

    Internet Experience:

    Information Problem-Solving Skills:

    Other Characteristics:

2. **Determine Goals:** _What should the students know?_

    Educational Goal (based on standards or curriculum):

    Instructional Need (gap in students' knowledge or skill):

    Instructional Goal (skills to be performed):

3. **Create Objectives:** *How will students achieve these goals and demonstrate what they've learned?* Fill in the table below to include objectives for the lesson or activity. Specify skills that students are expected to achieve to reach the goal of the lesson or activity. Use the following directions to help you fit each objective into the larger lesson:

- **Content:** If the objective relates to a certain content area (e.g., science, math, language arts, etc.), record the content area in this column.
- **Big6™:** If the objective relates to one or more steps in the information problem-solving process, place the corresponding Big6 step in this column.
- **Target:** If the objective relates directly to the ultimate goal, place a check-mark in this column.
- **Enabling:** If the objective relates to skills that must be met before a target objective can be performed, place a check-mark in this column (e.g., this may include basic Internet skills).
- **Internet Use:** If the objective calls for use of the Internet, indicate the types of Internet functions that would be appropriate: information resources (e.g., view Web sites for information), communications technology (e.g., e-mail), or presentation tool (e.g., creation of Web page).

Objective: Include required *behavior, conditions* under which they must be performed, and *criteria* by which each performance must be completed.	Content	Big6™ (include step)	Target	Enabling	Internet Use

4. **Plan Activities and Select Media:** *How can I plan a lesson using the Internet that will help students achieve the objectives?*

   Create a lesson plan including:
   - ☐ Subject
   - ☐ Unit
   - ☐ Topic
   - ☐ Audience
   - ☐ Goal
   - ☐ Purpose
   - ☐ Prerequisites
   - ☐ Objectives (content area and Big6)
   - ☐ Activities
   - ☐ Materials
   - ☐ Student evaluation

   Media Selection:
   What tools can be used to *deliver* instruction (must support objectives and other characteristics and logistics)?
   - ☐ Overhead projector
   - ☐ Blackboard/whiteboard
   - ☐ Internet
   - ☐ Video
   - ☐ Audio
   - ☐ Print materials (worksheets, etc.)
   - ☐ People (other school staff, community members, etc.)
   - ☐ None
   - ☐ Other (explain): _____

5. **Organize Materials and Resources:** *How do I prepare to carry out the lesson?*
   The following are some suggestions for preparing activities, materials and resources for a given lesson. Feel free to add original ideas.

   Resource Selection:
   - ☐ Save Web sites in a "bookmark" or "favorites" file.
   - ☐ Gather print and electronic resources to display or distribute during lesson.

   Resource Creation:
   - ☐ Create a Web page with information and resource lists pertaining to the lesson.
   - ☐ Create student print or electronic workbooks or worksheets to guide students through objectives.

   Presentation:
   - ☐ Create an outline for the presentation of information during the lesson.
   - ☐ Develop a presentation using computer-based presentation software (e.g., Microsoft *PowerPoint*).
   - ☐ Upload the presentation to the Web.

Communication:

☐ Contact other organizations (e.g., classes, telementoring programs) to set up Internet communication activities.

☐ Set up electronic mailing list for the class.

Logistics:

☐ Staff should be trained or should have relevant professional experience in Internet skills for a particular lesson.

☐ Room is reserved.

☐ Equipment and resources are available and ready to use.

☐ Acceptable use policies are established and parental permission is received.

6. **Set Agenda:** *How do I carry out my plan?*

Use this space to create an agenda for lesson activities. (Feel free to make copies of this page for additional days or sessions or recreate on to a separate page for more writing space.)

DAY/SESSION _____

Objectives:

Activities:

DAY/SESSION _____

Objectives:

Activities:

DAY/SESSION _____

Objectives:

Activities:

---

7. **Evaluate Instruction:** *How can I improve next time?*
The following questions may be answered after instruction to help information mentors plan for the next lesson or activity.

■ How well did the students achieve the objectives? What areas were weakest?

■ What actions did I take in planning that can be eliminated next time?

■ What actions did I leave out that I should include next time?

■ What worked and what didn't work during the delivery of instruction?

■ What additional training or practice do I require in order to more efficiently integrate the Internet into instruction?

■ Other observations:

Planning Instruction Using the Internet

Worksheet 1
Sample Completed Worksheet

Lesson or Activity Profile

Subject Area: <u>Social Studies</u>

Unit: <u>Immigration (to U.S.)</u>

Topic: <u>Countries of Immigrants</u>

Grade Level: <u>5</u>

Planning Steps

> **Planning Instruction at a Glance**
> 1. Assess Learners
> 2. Determine Goals
> 3. Create Objectives
> 4. Plan Activities and Select Media
> 5. Organize Materials and Resources
> 6. Set Agenda
> 7. Evaluate Instruction

1. **Assess Learners:** *What do the students currently know?*
   Subject Knowledge or Experience: <u>Students have already learned about the different cultural backgrounds of people living in the U.S.</u>

   Internet Experience: <u>Students know how to use the computer and can log on to the Internet. Students have done some searching.</u>

   Information Problem-Solving Skills: <u>No previous knowledge of Big6, but students have identified questions within pre-written paragraphs and have organized note cards into Venn diagrams (Synthesis).</u>

   Other Characteristics: <u>Students work best when they have specific guidelines and can work together to search for information.</u>

2. **Determine Goals:** *What should the students know?*

   Educational Goal (based on standards or curriculum): <u>Understand different perspectives of U.S. citizens.</u>

Instructional Need (gap in students' knowledge or skill): <u>Students understand the basic differences between people of different cultures, but they don't understand where and how people lived before they moved to the United States.</u>

Instructional Goal (skills to be performed): <u>Students will create a project about a specific country in which a U.S. immigrant previously lived.</u>

3. **Create Objectives:** *How will students achieve these goals and demonstrate what they've learned?* Fill in the table below to include objectives for the lesson or activity. Specify skills that students are expected to achieve to reach the goal of the lesson or activity. Use the following directions to help you fit each objective into the larger lesson:

■ **Content:** If the objective relates to a certain content area (e.g., science, math, language arts, etc.), record the content area in this column.

■ **Big6™:** If the objective relates to one or more steps in the information problem-solving process, place the corresponding Big6 step in this column.

■ **Target:** If the objective relates directly to the ultimate goal, place a check-mark in this column.

■ **Enabling:** If the objective relates to skills that must be met before a target objective can be performed, place a check-mark in this column (e.g., this may include basic Internet skills).

■ **Internet Use:** If the objective calls for use of the Internet, indicate the types of Internet functions that would be appropriate: information resources (e.g., view Web sites for information), communications technology (e.g., e-mail), or presentation tool (e.g., creation of Web page).

Objective: Include required *behavior, conditions* under which they must be performed, and *criteria* by which each performance must be completed.	Content	Big6™ (include step)	Target	Enabling	Internet Use
1. Assess information on the Web to determine its quality and authenticity.		Step 4 – Use of Info		✔	✔
2. Narrow information searches in order to locate relevant information about the country.		Step 3 – Location & Access			
3. Interview an immigrant to the U.S.	✔	Step 3 – Location & Access	✔		✔ e-mail option
4. Take notes on specific aspects of the country included on assignment sheet.	✔	Step 4 – Use of Info	✔		
5. Create visual and audio presentation and	✔	Step 5 – Synthesis		✔	

4. **Plan Activities and Select Media:** *How can I plan a lesson using the Internet that will help students achieve the objectives?*

Create a lesson plan including:
- ✔ Subject
- ✔ Unit
- ✔ Topic
- ✔ Audience
- ✔ Goal
- ✔ Purpose
- ✔ Prerequisites
- ✔ Objectives (content area and Big6)
- ✔ Activities
- ✔ Materials
- ✔ Student evaluation
- ✔ Other <u>Also, created an outline for kids including subject, goal, and requirements for research and presentation.</u>

Media Selection:
What tools can be used to *deliver* instruction (must support objectives and other characteristics and logistics)?
- ☐ Overhead projector
- ☑ Blackboard/whiteboard
- ☑ Internet <u>(one-on-one instruction)</u>
- ☑ Video <u>(presenting research chart)</u>
- ☐ Audio
- ☑ Print materials (worksheets, etc.) <u>Research charts are posted around classroom for the whole lesson as examples</u>
- ☑ People (other school staff, community members, etc.) <u>invite immigrants to class for practice interviews</u>
- ☐ None
- ☐ Other (explain):

5. **Organize Materials and Resources:** *How do I prepare to carry out the lesson?*
The following are some suggestions for preparing activities, materials and resources for a given lesson. Feel free to add original ideas.

Resource Selection:
- ☑ Save Web sites in a "bookmark" or "favorites" file.
- ☑ Gather print and electronic resources to display or distribute during lesson. <u>Print articles.</u>

Resource Creation:
- ☐ Create a Web page with information and resource lists pertaining to the lesson.
- ☑ Create student print or electronic workbooks or worksheets to guide students through objectives.

Presentation:
- ☑ Create an outline for the presentation of information during lesson.
- ☐ Develop a computer-based presentation using presentation software (e.g., Microsoft *PowerPoint*).
- ☐ Upload the presentation to the Web.

Communication:
- ☐ Contact other organizations (e.g., classes, telementoring programs) to set up Internet communication activities.
- ☑ Set up electronic mailing list for the class.

Logistics:
- ☐ Staff should be trained or should have relevant professional experience in Internet skills for a particular lesson. <u>Could use more practice in Internet searching.</u>
- ☑ Room is reserved.
- ☑ Equipment and resources are available and ready to use.
- ☐ Acceptable use policies are established and parental permission is received. <u>Will work with principal on this.</u>

6. **Set Agenda:** *How do I carry out my plan?*
   Use this space to create an agenda for lesson activities. (Feel free to make copies of this page for additional days or sessions or recreate onto a separate page for more writing space.)

DAY/SESSION <u>   1   </u>

Objectives:
3. Interview U.S. immigrant.

Activities:
Students interview immigrant and take notes.

DAY/SESSION <u>   2   </u>

Objectives:
4. Take notes on specific aspects of country on assignment sheet.

Activities: Each student chooses three topics to research, relating to immigrant's life in country of origin (e.g. government, food, and religion) and record questions about the topics.

---

7. **Evaluate Instruction:** *How can I improve next time?*
   The following questions may be answered after instruction to help information mentors plan for the next lesson or activity.

   ■ How well did the students achieve the objectives? What areas were weakest? <u>Students still need practice searching for information. Papers were not as well organized as I'd like. Students seemed to spend more time on making their presentations aesthetically pleasing.</u>

   ■ What actions did I take in planning that can be eliminated next time?

   ■ What actions did I leave out that I should include next time? <u>Look for more Internet resources at students' reading and comprehension level.</u>

   ■ What worked and what didn't work during the delivery of instruction? <u>Next time, spend more time on research methods and organizing paper.</u>

   ■ What additional training or practice do I require in order to more efficiently integrate the Internet into instruction? <u>Would like training in evaluating Internet sites and finding better sites for students.</u>

   ■ Other observations: <u>Should do two separate projects: one on research methods and one on writing the paper.</u>

Chapter Summary

- Internet use in education has several advantages but also presents some challenges.
- The Internet is not always an appropriate tool for a given lesson or activity.
- Educators and others should use a systematic approach to planning instruction to decide if, when, where, and how to incorporate Internet use.
- Systematic planning, based on instructional design principles, assists educators in planning effective instruction using these steps:
  1. Assess Learners
  2. Determine Goals
  3. Create Objectives
  4. Plan Activities and Select Media
  5. Organize Materials and Resources
  6. Set Agenda
  7. Evaluate Instruction
- Big6 Skills and Internet (technology) skills should be incorporated into content-area objectives by focusing on specific information problem-solving or technical skills as needed.

Chapter Pathfinder

Chapter 1—Planning Instruction Using the Internet

Internet Resources

AskERIC

http://www.askeric.org/

AskERIC is the award-winning Internet-based education information service of the Educational Resources Information Center (ERIC) System, headquartered at the ERIC Clearinghouse on Information & Technology and part of the School of Information Studies at Syracuse University. AskERIC components include an Internet-based question/answer service addressing issues in educational research; the "Virtual Library," a collection of resources including lesson plans, topical guides and access to the ERIC database; and "Research and Development," a team that uses cutting-edge technology to help AskERIC bring high-quality information services to the education community.

ED's Oasis

http://www.edsoasis.org/

This site, funded by AT&T's Education Foundation, and sponsored by the California Instructional Technology Clearinghouse, is designed to "help teachers use the Internet as an integral tool for teaching and learning." It contains links to educational Web sites for students and teachers, spotlight interviews with teachers using the Internet in the classroom, teacher resources, Web site evaluation guidelines, and information on ED's Oasis' electronic discussion list.

GEM—The Gateway to Educational Materials

http://www.thegateway.org

The GEM online catalog provides "one-stop, any-stop" access to high-quality Internet lesson plans, curriculum units, and other education resources. Visitors to the GEM site can search by: full-text, subject, keyword, or title, and can limit their search by grade or education level. But, the best feature of all is that items retrieved from a search, link directly to the Internet resources they describe.

ICONnect Curriculum Connections

http://www.ala.org/ICONN/curricu2.html

Developed by the ICONnect initiative of American Association of School Librarians (a division of American Library Association), this site provides links to Internet resources that can be integrated into the K-12 curriculum.

Mid-Continent Regional Educational Laboratory: Connections+

http://www.mcrel.org/connect/plus/index.html

This site consists of lesson plans, activities, and curriculum resources on the Internet linked with corresponding subject-area content standards. (From "Content Knowledge: A Compendium of Standards and Benchmarks for K-12 Education" http://www.mcrel.org/standards-benchmarks/)

Teacher/Pathfinder
http://teacherpathfinder.org/
Teacher/Pathfinder, an "educational Internet village," is designed to help teachers and others use resources on the Internet. Features include links to content-related Internet sites, resources for professional development and a search engine.

Virtual Reference Desk (VRD) AskA+ Locator
http://www.vrd.org/locator/index.html
The AskA+ Locator is a database of high-quality "AskA" services that link students, teachers, parents, and other members of the K-12 education community to subject area "experts." There are profiles for each AskA service that include: a general description of the service, the intended audience, the subject scope for that AskA service, links to that service's home page, e-mail address, contact person, and publisher. The user can search by: subject, keyword, grade level, or alphabetical list.

ERIC Citations

Eisenberg, M. B., & Johnson, D. (1996). Computer skills for information problem-solving: Learning and teaching technology in context. *ERIC Digest*. Syracuse, NY: ERIC Clearinghouse on Information and Technology. 6pp. (ED 392 463) [Online]. Available: *http://www.ed.gov/databases/ERIC_Digests/ed392463.html*
Over the past 20 years, library media professionals have worked to move from teaching isolated library skills to teaching integrated information skills. Effective integration of information skills has two requirements: (1) the skills must directly relate to the content area curriculum and to classroom assignments; and (2) the skills themselves need to be tied together in a logical and systematic information process model. Schools seeking to move from isolated computer skills instruction also need to focus on these requirements. Library media specialists, computer teachers, and classroom teachers need to work together to develop units and lessons that will include both computer skills, general information skills, and content-area curriculum outcomes. The "Big Six Skills Approach to Information Problem Solving" is an information literacy curriculum, an information problem-solving process, and a set of skills that provide a strategy for effectively and efficiently meeting information needs. This model is transferable to school, personal, and work applications, as well as all content areas and the full range of grade levels. The Big Six Skills include: (1) task definition; (2) information seeking strategies; (3) location and access; (4) use of information; (5) synthesis; and (6) evaluation. An addendum is included which presents skills and knowledge related to technology that are not part of the computer and information technology curriculum. Contains 24 references.

Morgan, N. A., & Sprague, C. (Ed.). (2000). An introduction to Internet resources for K-12 educators. Part I: Information resources, Update 2000. *ERIC Digest*, Syracuse, NY: ERIC Clearinghouse on Information and Technology. 2pp. (ED number pending). Through state and regional education networks and commercial providers, the vast resources of the Internet are increasingly available to administrators, school library media specialists, and classroom teachers. This ERIC Digest lists a sample of no-cost Internet resources of special interest to K-12 educators (resources and addresses are subject to change). Highlights include: guides to Internet resources, lesson plans and teaching materials, keypals and penpals, acceptable use policies, technology plans for K-12 schools, Internet projects for the classroom, grant information, e-rate information, federal government information, state education departments, standards-based education, reference resources, library catalogs, and other resources.

Morgan, N. A., & Sprague, C. (Ed.). (2000). An introduction to Internet resources for K-12 educators. Part II: Question answering, listservs, discussion groups, Update 2000. *ERIC Digest*, Syracuse, NY: ERIC Clearinghouse on Information and Technology. 2pp. (ED number pending). As K-12 schools connect to the Internet, a new method of communication opens up to educators and their students. This ERIC Digest describes some sample services and resources that are available to the K-12 community by electronic mail over the Internet. Question answering services, listservs, and usenet newsgroups are listed.

Provenzo Jr., E. F. (1998). *Educator's brief guide to the Internet and the World Wide Web*. Larchmont, NY: Eye on Education. 182 pp. (ED 421 975). This book is an introduction to the Internet and World Wide Web for educators. The purpose is to provide a practical handbook for administrators and teachers, as well as to reflect on the potential of this new technology to redefine the traditional curriculum in elementary and high schools. Throughout this book appear boxed definitions and highlighted Internet site addresses that pertain to the text. The guide includes the following sections: (1) "Introduction"; (2) "Getting Connected to the Internet"; (3) "The Internet and Education"; (4) "Integrating the Internet into the Curriculum"; (5) "Model Internet Lesson Plans"; (6) "Electronic Mail"; (7) "Establishing an Acceptable Use Policy for Your School"; (8) "Learning about Others through the Internet"; (9) "Useful Web Sites for Teachers"; (10) "Setting up Your Own Web Site"; and (11) "Just for Fun." The appendices include a partially annotated bibliography (47 titles), sample acceptable use policies and forms, and an index to terms defined in the book.

Sharp, V. F., Levine, M. G., & Sharp, R. M. (1996). *The best web sites for teachers*. Eugene, OR: International Society for Technology in Education. 353pp. (ED 417 712). This book identifies more than 650 Internet and World Wide Web sites across the K-12 curriculum that can benefit teachers who may not have time to carry out lengthy searches themselves. The Web sites in this book are organized alphabetically by the following K-12 subject areas: art, bilingual education, drama, ESL, foreign language, health education and physical education, journalism, language arts, math, music, science, social studies, special education, and vocational and technical education. Within each subject area, the sites are organized into at least one of three categories: lesson plans, other resources, and museums and exhibits. The sites described may include a wide range of materials—lesson plans and pictures that can be printed out, online multimedia presentations for students; interactive games; weekly brain teasers; searchable activities; databases for teachers; contests; pen pal opportunities; forms; downloadable graphics; videos; and other resources that can enrich the K-12 curriculum. Appendix 1 describes Web sites for newsgroups, that allow teachers to read and post messages, as well as listservs through which teachers can subscribe to electronic newsletters. Appendix 2 lists Web sites for information on search tools and Appendix 3 provides some sample forms for evaluating recommended and new Web sites.

Stoloff, D. L. (1998). Developing educational signposts on the World Wide Web: A school-university cooperative curriculum project. 52 pp. (ED 418 920). This project's goal was to develop a network of educational signposts and electronic textbooks to support K-12 student learning and curriculum articulation across eastern Connecticut, and to enhance teacher education and graduate programs at Eastern Connecticut State University (ECSU). Through support from an AAUP-CSU grant, selected ECSU graduate students who were also K-12 teachers in the region attended a summer workshop that focused on the development of Web pages for the World Wide Web and commitment to integrating the World Wide Web into their curriculum. Participants learned how to use the World Wide Web and how to create home pages and electronic text. They developed a variety of electronic textbooks and school home pages. Project linkage titles included: "Find it on the World Wide Web," "Online Resources for Educators New to the Internet," "K12Links," "Curriculum Enhancement," "Newspapers in Education," "Glen Lessig's Education Technology Bookmarks," "Arline Mykietyn's Bookmarks on Harriet Tubman," "J.P.'s Eclectic Bookmarks," and "Mrs. Wargo's Bookmarks WJJS Media Center."

Tate, N. A. (1998). *Getting elementary educators caught up in the web.* (In: "SITE 98: Society for Information Technology & Teacher Education International Conference (9th, Washington, DC, March 10-14, 1998) Proceedings"), 7 pp. (ED 421 158). This paper describes the development and implementation of a World Wide Web training session for educators in a local elementary school. A K-12 World Wide Web Educator's listserv proved to be invaluable in obtaining suggestions for Web-based curriculum resources that K-12 educators had reviewed and evaluated. Washburn University's (Topeka, Kansas) computing lab was chosen for the hands-on training. A written reference manual was provided for the teachers to take away with them. Goals of this teacher inservice training were three-fold: (1) to provide background information on the Web and search techniques; (2) to increase the teachers' awareness of the multitude of curriculum resources already available on the Internet for K-6 educators; (3) to have the teachers create a simple, Web-based activity using a Web authoring tool. The schedule of events is outlined, and teacher feedback comments and critical success factors are listed.

Technology & innovations in education/Mid-Continent Regional Educational Lab (1998). *Facing the challenge of technology integration. A portfolio of processes. Facilitator's manual.* 90pp., Rapid City, SD: Aurora, CO. (ED 421 983). The overall goal of this technology integration work is to identify the content and processes vital to decision making as schools transform education through technology integration. This guide includes a collection of content and process strategies to start the learner on the path. It contains the following sections: (1) Professional Development Model; (2) Using Processes Portfolios to Guide Decision Making; (3) Strategy: Framework Analysis; (4) Framework for Education; (5) Indicators of an Open, Networked Learning Environment; (6) Learning in Cyberspace; (7) Technology Integration Portfolio; (8) Building a Sound Knowledge Base—includes worksheets and handouts for presentation; (9) Changing Mental Modes—includes worksheets and handouts for presentation; (10) Teaching & Learning—includes worksheets and handouts for presentation; (11) Classroom & Systems Connections—includes worksheets and handouts for presentation; and (12) References. Also included are two *PowerPoint* Sound Technology Integration disks (one for Windows and one for Macintosh).

Wilson, L. (1997-1998). Testing the water before surfing. Technology in the classroom. *Childhood Education, 74* (2), 116-17. (EJ 557 316). Claims that although teachers are increasingly expected to integrate technology—particularly the Internet—into their classrooms, it is the exceptional school system that prepares its teachers to use the Internet appropriately. Describes new products and resources that facilitate constructive and relatively easy use of the Internet, including the "Learning Online" series, CD-ROMs, and online encyclopedias.

Coaching K–12 Students with the Internet

Coaching K–12 Students with the Internet

Chapter Profile

Once students are faced with an information problem that requires Internet use (such as a homework assignment or research project), information mentors can help them navigate the Internet within the Big6 framework. Information mentors in this role may include parents, technology teachers, library media specialists, classroom teachers, and other students. This chapter presents issues involved when using the Internet with K-12 students and offers suggestions for successful information mentoring experiences.

Guide individual K-12 students or classes in their use of the Internet for information problem-solving while maximizing safety, responsibility, and effectiveness.

To guide K-12 students in using the Internet, information mentors need to be able to:
1. Connect to, search, and communicate using the Internet.
2. Provide Internet access.
3. Understand steps of Big6 process.

This chapter will prepare you to:
1. Understand the importance of guiding students in using the Internet at school and at home.
2. Identify areas of the Big6 process where information mentors can help students use the Internet to reach academic goals.
3. Establish guidelines for appropriate and responsible Internet use.
4. Identify issues in using the Internet with K-12 students at school and at home.
5. Guide students in using the Internet within the Big6 process.

Providing Guidance at School and Home

Although K-12 students may already have many skills necessary to use Internet tools, they may still require guidance when using those tools within an information problem-solving process. Students may be able to find Web sites of their favorite rock groups and talk with friends in chat rooms as well as locate information for school projects, but it's important to make sure they view the Internet as part of the big picture of information resources and solutions. Information mentors can help students develop their information literacy skills by coaching their use of the Internet at school and at home.

Coaching at School

Aiding students in their use of the Internet may be included as part of a class lesson where the Internet is a recommended or required tool for achieving a defined task. Classroom teachers, technology teachers, library media specialists, and other staff may act as coaches during the school day or after school for students who require assistance with browsing or searching the Web, using e-mail programs, developing Web pages, or other related activities.

Internet coaching may include one-on-one assistance with individual students or a more structured group instruction session. Darrow (1999) offers suggestions for teachers and library media specialists to help students find, organize, and evaluate information from the Web using the Big6. For instance, he offers the following suggestions to students for selecting Web sites during the Location & Access stage (after a search has been conducted) (adapted from Darrow, 1999, p. 10):

1. Read and scan the "front page" of several Web sites from search results and decide whether or not the site contains any information for the particular topic
2. If not, look at the next Web site in the list of results
3. If yes, bookmark the page and then go back to the list of results
4. Repeat this process until an adequate number of Web sites is found.

Tomei (1996) suggests providing students with a workbook that contains questions relating to the lesson objectives that can be answered at previously selected Web sites. This exercise focuses on the Use of Information step of the Big6. The workbook can also contain questions relating to the effectiveness of the lesson, focusing on the Evaluation step of the Big6.

Coaching at Home

Of course, many of the tips for using the Internet at school may be applied when using the Internet at home. Parents can serve as information mentors at home by helping their children use the Internet for school assignments and projects. While helping children with homework is not a new concept for parents, new skills are demanded by the Internet's set of tools. Many parents have yet to master these new skills. As parents learn Internet skills in combination with the information problem-solving process, parents can offer their children invaluable life lessons.

Information Mentor Spotlight: Parents

The National Education Goals for the year 2000 (Goals 2000: Educate America Act) highlights the importance of parental involvement in education: "Every school will promote partnerships that will increase parental involvement and participation in promoting the social, emotional, and academic growth of children" (U.S. Congress 1994). One way parents can get involved is by helping their children complete school assignments and conduct research using information tools and resources, such as the Internet.

Parents play many special roles in their children's learning. By engaging in learning activities themselves—such as reading, taking a class, or searching the Internet—they act as role models for lifelong learning. By showing an interest in their children's homework and school assignments, parents demonstrate that their children's academic success is important and this interest can motivate students to perform well (Paulu, 1995). By helping their children complete assignments, parents can act as coaches, leading students through the entire information problem-solving process: from clarifying a research question to providing access to necessary resources, to editing a final product (Eisenberg & Berkowitz, 1996).

Why Use the Internet at Home?

Although many schools provide Internet access to students, it is valuable to emphasize Internet use in other contexts, including at home or in the public library (Eisenberg & Berkowitz, 1996). First, children may not have enough time in school to fully explore Internet features. Second, children should be aware that the Internet may be used for many different purposes (including school, recreation, and career). Finally, children can sharpen their critical-thinking skills by learning to evaluate all kinds of information resources, including those found on the Internet.

Many families are connecting to the Internet; according to a study by Emerging Technologies Research, the number of U.S. households using the Internet or an online service increased from 3.1 million in 1994 to 15.1 million in 1996. Though the number of Internet connections is rising, the study states that much of this Internet use is limited to e-mail communication, news, and personal research (Miller, 1997). It is unclear how many families are using the Internet to complete school assignments at home.

It is important that all types of information mentors and students use Internet-based information and tools in the larger context of systematic information problem-solving. This chapter suggests ways that information mentors can coach students through the Big6 Skills to complete school assignments, using the Internet when appropriate.

Examples of Parent-Child Internet Interactions

The most popular Internet activities that involve parent and child interaction normally center around the Location & Access and Use of Information steps of the Big6. Guidance also occurs frequently at the Synthesis stage. Some examples include the following (these examples were gathered in part from responses to a posting to the ChildrenFirst e-mail discussion group of the National PTA):

Location & Access:

- **Searching**—Parents provide assistance with searching the Internet for information on any variety of topics, from coral reefs, to facts about France, to second-hand smoke. Parents can assist children with using search engines and generating search terms.
- **Navigating**—When students are unfamiliar with a Web browser, parents can help them learn to use the navigational and organizational functions such as the front and back button, bookmarks, location bar, etc.

In the following example[3], a parent lets her 7th-grade daughter explore the Internet on her own (i.e., "driving the mouse") before stepping in to help (Bowman, personal communication, 1999):

> Erin had a social studies assignment to research information on Chile and to do an oral presentation with visual aids. When conducting her research, Erin used the Internet on her own for the first time. With her mother's permission, Erin used her mother's password to access her family's Internet account at home. She spent several hours online trying to find information on Chile. Although she found very little information, she learned a lot about the types of information resources available on the Internet. After some time, Erin's mother aided her in searching for information and found several useful resources for Erin to use in her project. Erin's mother explained what a search engine is and how different search engines work. They reviewed the search results together to decide which links most likely contained the information needed for the project. At the end of the searching session, Erin was satisfied not only because she found information for her project, but because she learned how to use search engines, create and reword search terms, decode search results, and navigate the Web using Web browser buttons. With new skills and confidence, Erin now uses the Internet more frequently for fun as well as school research.

Use of Information:

- **Transferring information**—Parents can assist children to "move" Internet-based content into environments that allow better interactivity with the information (e.g., copying and pasting sections into word processing files, printing out information). It is important to note that along with transferring information from the Internet, parents should assist children in properly citing original sources and asking permission when necessary. (See Appendix F: Citing Internet Sources.)
- **Monitoring information use**—Parents can help children identify quality information resources on the Internet by observing their Internet use and pointing out accurate vs. inaccurate information, valid vs. invalid sources, etc.
- **Communication**—Creating an open environment for discussion allows parents and children to address issues like information quality and safety on the Internet. Information mentors can apply "teachable moments" that result from newspaper or magazine articles, television programs and other everyday experiences (McCombs, 1999).

---

3   Names of students have been changed in all examples.

One parent describes her experience helping her young son "weed" through questionable sites.

> When Jordan did a report on Walt Disney, he came across a site that said Disney was alive and well on another planet. Although the article started off with legitimate information, it ended up taking a left turn (McCombs, 1999).

In this situation, a parent can explain that a resource that contains inaccurate information is considered unacceptable.

Synthesis:

- **Compile information**—As children prepare their final products, parents can guide them in synthesizing information from a variety of Internet and non-Internet sources.

> Andrew needed to collect 100 facts about France for a 5th-grade assignment. He used Yahoo! to find several Web sites with information about France. After Andrew printed out some Web pages and jotted down some interesting facts, his father helped him identify different categories (e.g., history, culture, geography, etc.) for the information, so he could organize his list. Andrew's father also helped him record information on the Web sites cited for the bibliography.

- **Creating the final product**—Parents can also guide children in creating their projects, which can include print-based reports, posters as well as online newsletters, Web pages, and online presentations.

Using the Internet with K-12 Students

Several issues must be considered when using the Internet with K-12 students whether at home or at school.

Provide access: There are two general ways to establish access to the Internet: through modems and through direct connections (Simpson & McElmeel, 1997). When connecting from home, one would most likely connect through a modem attached to a personal computer. This would require installation of communications software, an account with an Internet service provider, and, of course, a phone line.

Schools can also connect to the Internet using a modem. Many schools, however, connect to the Internet through a direct connection (via a special digital line purchased from the local telecommunications company), allowing for quicker access and convenience (Simpson and McElmeel, 1997). Technical expertise is required to set up and maintain the digital line system.

If at all possible, parents should provide Internet access from a home computer. If it is impossible to connect to the Internet from home, parents should make sure that their children can use a computer with Internet access after school hours, whether it is at a public library, community center, or friend's house (Eisenberg & Berkowitz, 1996).

Online Safety

This remains the biggest concern for many parents and educators who are responsible for children's use of the Internet. It is true that many Web pages, newsgroup messages, and other sources contain content that is inappropriate for children. These challenges can be viewed as opportunities to set policies and rules for children regarding acceptable use of the Internet at home, school, and other locations. This will not only help students develop a sense of responsibility, but will help sharpen their critical thinking skills as they evaluate the quality of resources. Some common solutions for monitoring safety include:

- **Policies:** Many school districts have Acceptable Use Policies (AUP) to establish "standards for responsible conduct" on the Internet (Palgi, 1996, 32). Similar agreements may be made between parents and children at home to outline what is and is not appropriate, what actions to take when a child encounters inappropriate material, and what rules to follow for sharing information with others online (see Online Safety Project, 1998). (Additional resources are included in Appendix G: Online Safety).

- **Guided use:** Adults can monitor children's use of the Internet by observing them as they navigate the Web and read online materials. This is especially helpful for younger children who may not have developed the evaluation skills necessary to differentiate appropriate from inappropriate materials on their own.

- **Blocking/filtering:** There are a number of software products that claim to block access to pornographic or otherwise offensive materials that may be unsuitable for children. The issue of using such software products has been quite controversial. Some favor the use of Internet filters because they can reduce the risk that children will access "inappropriate" materials, therefore reducing liability for libraries and schools and allowing parents to feel more at ease with home Internet use. (For example, some parents choose to enable parental controls available through Internet Service Providers such as America Online that allow them to create special accounts for children that limit access to certain sites.) Critics of filtering claim that current products are unable to function with complete accuracy, therefore censoring acceptable materials and exposing children to the very materials they intended to block. (For a list of resources on this complicated issue, please see Appendix G.)

- **Computer in public area:** The placement of computers in a room can help determine the degree to which adults can observe and interact with children using the Internet. For instance, some families place the computer in the family room where issues can be discussed and information shared openly, and some school library media centers place computer stations in the middle of the room where library media specialists, teachers and other school staff can easily monitor student use of the Internet.

Quality

It doesn't take much browsing or searching for people to learn that they can't believe everything they read on the Internet. Potentially anyone with Internet access can publish a Web page and claim to be an expert on a certain subject. It is no doubt challenging to weed through the junk that is available, but armed with a solid Web page assessment rubric, adults and children alike can learn to distinguish the good from the garbage with greater ease. Some criteria to consider when assessing a Web site include:

- **Reliability of source:** Who is the author or publisher of the site? Is it from a well-known organization such as NASA, the Smithsonian Institution, or Sea World/Busch Gardens? Is it an individual's home page? If so, is there information on the author's qualifications posted on the site? Is there a possibility of bias due to commercial, political or other interests?

- **Accuracy:** Regardless of the reliability of an Internet source, it is a good idea to verify facts with a second source (another reliable Web page, magazine article, or encyclopedia).
- **Age-appropriateness:** There are very few sites written for young children on the Internet. Some Web sites contain inappropriate materials (as discussed above), while some simply contain language and concepts that are too advanced for young Internet users. It is important that educators, parents, and other information mentors review sites for age appropriateness before sharing them with students, just as they would with any other type of information resource.

See Chapter 4 for further discussion of Web site evaluation criteria and see Appendix C for a list of resources on evaluating Web sites.

Copyright

Although it is sometimes more difficult to identify authorship information in electronic sources, it is important to note that creators of any print material own the copyright to their work as soon as it's posted. This includes material published on the Internet. Citing sources and requesting permission are important practices for educators who incorporate others' materials in their instruction and for students who use Web-based information in reports or other projects. Downloading complete Web sites or complete pages should be avoided. When in doubt, ask permission from the original author or creator of Web site contents and e-mail messages.

Be careful when:
- Cutting and pasting sections of a Web page
- Paraphrasing information in reports and other assignments
- Re-posting e-mail messages written by others as personal communication or public electronic discussion.

When publishing or posting work on the Internet, consider:
- Including copyright notices and statements regarding permission to use your work, and register your material with the Copyright Office (Bruwelheide, 1995).[4]
- Getting permission from students or others whose original work will be included in the resource.

See Simpson, 1997, p. 113 for "Copyright and Plagiarism Guidelines for Students." See Appendix F for resources on citing Internet resources.

Information Mentor Internet Proficiency

Some educators and parents may be thinking, "How can I assist students with their use of the Internet if I don't even know how to navigate the Internet myself?" If you are still trying to find the onramp to the "information superhighway," you are not alone. There are many resources designed to help people get started using this exciting collection of resources, including:

---

4 According to the Berne Convention for the Protection of Literary and Artistic Works, creators of Internet materials automatically own the copyright to their work. Although copyright notices are not required, they will protect one's rights as a copyright holder in case any dispute should occur (Simpson, 1997).

- **Workshops and training sessions:** Educators may attend in-service workshops and other training opportunities. Some school districts offer Internet training to parents as well. For instance, the Nueva School in Hillsborough, California, holds "Parent Internet Driving School" workshops during parent-conference days. During these workshops, parents learn Internet skills and are introduced to the same Internet-related activities their children are learning (see Abilock, 1997).
- **Online courses:** For information mentors who have made the first step in connecting to the Internet, there are some courses administered through e-mail and the Web to help people improve their Internet skills. For instance, the American Library Association offers a set of online lessons called FamiliesConnect to help "parents, grandparents, and other extended family members learn about the Internet and how to use it with children and for their own personal information needs" *(http://www.ala.org/ICONN/fc-course.html)*.
- **Written guides and other information:** Many books, articles, pamphlets, and other resources provide basic tips and background for Internet beginners. For a list of resources to help information mentors get started on their Internet adventures, see Appendix A.

Guidelines and Examples: Homework Scenario

This section presents a sample homework scenario that involves Internet use, and provides suggestions for completing the assignment using the Big6. This scenario highlights parents as information mentors, but the type of guidance described can be offered by educators and other information mentors as well.

Example: Research Project

Robyn, an eighth-grade student, comes home from school with an English/Global Studies research project—to present multiple views on a current controversial topic. Her teacher provided a list of possible final products (e.g., paper, and poster, Web page). Students are required to present their products to the class. Robyn is frustrated and confused about where to start. What would you do to help her complete the project with as little stress as possible?

Big6™ Steps and Research Project

1. Big6 Step 1—Task Definition
Robyn is unable to identify a clear information problem, because she is having trouble focusing on a specific topic (a common situation). Robyn's parents try to help in the following ways:

Narrowing the topic:

- Discussion—Robyn's parents engage her in a conversation to elicit the types of topics that interest her. They ask if she feels particularly strongly about any recent topics in the news.
- Preliminary research—They encourage her to leaf through recent newspapers or magazines, watch television news programs, listen to news radio (e.g., National Public Radio), or visit news-related Internet sites, such as:

AP on the Globe Online:

http://www.boston.com/globe/cgi-bin/globe.cgi?ap/apnat.htm

CNN Interactive:

http://cnn.com/index.html

Current News (links to Internet news sources):

http://blair.library.rhodes.edu/Default1htmls/news.html#Newspapers

Identifying information needed:

Robyn's mother helps her understand that based on the instructions on her assignment sheet, Robyn needs opinions and facts on one issue, and the information must be current.

2. Big6 Step 2—Information Seeking Strategies

During the first step, Robyn narrows her topic to animal testing in medical research. Now, she creates a list of possible resources, including periodicals (print or electronic based), Internet sites from various organizations or groups for and against, people from various organizations (via face-to-face, telephone, or e-mail interviews), and any supporting documentation (statistics, research).

Robyn's mother reminds her to consult her school library media specialist, or to contact a digital reference service (see Chapter 3) to obtain information on appropriate sources. After Robyn creates a list of possible sources, her mother helps her to prioritize which sources are most appropriate. Robyn decides to begin with the periodical database in her school library media center.

3. Big6 Step 3—Location & Access

Searching:

After she collects some background articles on animal testing, Robyn decides to search the Web with her mother's assistance. She goes to the Web Crawler search engine (*http://webcrawler.com/*) and types in the words **animal testing medical research**. Wow! She is bombarded with 227,950 hits! This is way too many resources to skim through. Her mother suggests clicking the "Help" button at the top of the page to learn about searching techniques in WebCrawler. Once in the "Help" page, they click on "Basics of WebCrawler Searching." Here they read that you just need to type a series of words or a phrase in the query box. "Well, I *did* that," Robyn sighs. Her mother spots in small print, beneath the sample query box, a link for "search tips." This link takes them to a page with a more promising link, "Improving your Results." Under the section "focusing your search," they learn that placing quotation marks around the search phrase forces the search engine to return Web pages that contain the exact phrase, instead of pages that contain each individual word separately.

Robyn and her mom try their search again, this time with quotes around the phrase **"animal testing" "medical research."** A little better—only 2211 hits—but still way too many. They click on the "help" button again and choose "advanced searching." This page describes ways to narrow the search by adding the word "AND" between phrases. The search **"animal testing" AND "medical research"** yields 11 results. This is a very manageable number to review, and Robyn and her mother skim the document summaries to decide which ones to open. While reading the summaries, they notice that most sites clearly oppose animal testing. They skim through a couple sites and decide to try another search engine.

Robyn and her mother go to the Alta Vista search engine (*http://www.altavista.com*) and try this search string: **+"animal testing" +"medical research."** The "help" section suggests they should place quotes around phrases as they did in WebCrawler. They also found out that they should use plus signs in front of each phrase to request sites that contain both phrases. (This is similar to the way they used the word "AND" in WebCrawler).

The Alta Vista search yielded 37 results. Robyn and her mom skim through the summaries to decide which sites to check out. They decide to open the page titled "Animal Research Database" because it is from a university (noted by the extension "edu" in its address) and because it looks like it is in favor of using animals as models in medical research. They also decide to open a site called "Alternatives to Animal Use" from the Animal Care Council, because it appears to contain a different slant on the issue. After skimming some sites, Robyn learns that vivisection is a term used for animal experimentation. She decides to search later using this term.

Skimming:

Now Robyn is ready to check out a few of the sites from her search. First she clicks on "Animal Research Database." She immediately sees a large table of contents with several technical terms. Her mother suggests that she start by reading through the first few sections to get a basic idea. She decides to save this Web site in their bookmark file and move on. The next site clearly explains what information is provided. After following some of the links, Robyn and her mother are able to identify appropriate statements and passages. This viewing and skimming process continues until Robyn finds two good sites representing each view and one site discussing both views.

 Tips: For more help with Internet searching, see Appendix B: Searching the Internet.

4. Big6 Step 4—Use of Information

After Robyn identifies and skims the sites she wants to use, she is ready to read the sources more closely and take some notes. Since she is most comfortable working from paper, she decides to print out the Web pages. Quickly realizing that she is using up many sheets of paper, she copies and pastes the most helpful sections of each Web page into a word processing file that she later prints out.

Robyn's mother sees that this information originating from the Internet is now saved on her computer as an adaptable file. She reminds Robyn to copy down the title, Web address, and author's name for each Web site, the number of the paragraph on the page in which the passage was located, and the date she last accessed each Web page.

Once the pages are printed, Robyn uses her highlighter and pen to mark the most relevant information. Her mother suggests that she also write some notes on a blank piece of paper, so that it's easier to organize the ideas later.

 Internet tips: For more information about citing electronic sources, see Appendix F.

 For more information about evaluation of Web sites, see Appendix C.

5. Big6 Step 5—Synthesis

After viewing many Web sites on the subject of animal testing, Robyn concludes there should be a Web page that clearly presents arguments from all sides and points people to more information in print and on the Internet. She decides that her final product will be a Web page written especially for middle school students. She has a friend who can design Web sites using HTML, so all she needs to do is organize the information she wants to present. Her mother helps her create an outline specifying the structure of the page. She also helps Robyn stay focused on presenting her argument, instead of focusing on the graphics and links that will be added later.

> Internet tips: For more information on Web site design, see Appendix H.

6. Big6 Step 6—Evaluation

After Robyn's mother reads her paper (now a Web page draft), she suggests that Robyn needs to include more of her own views in the summary. Later, they discuss their experiences with the Internet and write down things that they want to remember the next time. They mentioned reading "help" sections of search engines and copying and pasting information from the Web into word processing documents as particularly effective strategies.

Followed in this way, the Big6 is a practical and rather natural approach to completing homework assignments, such as a research project. Robyn, with her mother's guidance, addressed each step as she went from deciding on a research topic to evaluating her completed paper. They found that the Internet had some helpful information, once they spent time learning the most effective search strategies. Robyn also used the Web's presentation features to post new content that communicates the results of her research for other students and Internet users.

Coaching Students on the Internet
Using the Big6™

Worksheet 2

Instructions: This worksheet is intended to help information mentors and students record decisions, problems, and solutions that occur while solving information problems using the Internet.[5] The notes you take can help you in future assignments. This worksheet encompasses the entire information problem-solving process but focuses specifically on Internet use. For problems encountered during the information problem-solving process, refer to a library media specialist for assistance. Feel free to move back and forth between Big6 steps and repeat steps during the course of the assignment.

1. **Big6 Step 1—Task Definition:** *What is the assignment? What is my topic?*

   How to Find Out
   Contact teacher or classmates to **clarify an assignment or discuss topics** by:
   ☐ E-mail
   ☐ Phone
   ☐ In-person discussion
   ☐ Videoconference
   ☐ Online chat

   Find information to help **narrow or expand an assignment topic** in:
   ☐ World Wide Web
   ☐ Journal articles
   ☐ Books (library catalog)
   ☐ Messages to experts
   ☐ Other sources

   Create your plan by completing the statements below:

   Original assignment: _____

   _____

   Date started: _____   Date due: _____

   Research question/topic **ideas** (can brainstorm on separate sheet): _____

   _____

   _____

   Refined question/topic: _____

   _____

---

5 Based on Eisenberg, Michael B. and Berkowitz, Robert E. (1996). Helping with Homework: A Parent's Guide to Information Problem Solving. Syracuse, NY: ERIC Clearinghouse on Information and Technology, Syracuse University.

Types of information needed (check all that apply):
- ☐ Facts
- ☐ Opinion
- ☐ Numerical information
- ☐ Other: _____

Format of final product:
- ☐ Report
- ☐ Poster
- ☐ Computer-based presentation
- ☐ Video
- ☐ Web page
- ☐ Brochure/pamphlet
- ☐ Other: _____

2. **Big6 Step 2—Information Seeking Strategies:** *What sources should I use? Which sources are the best?*

Review the list below and add any resources you think would help with your assignment or question. Next, place numbers to the left of each item to indicate which ones are most likely to help you, in order of priority (for instance, if you think you should talk to your school library media specialist first, place a "1" to the left of "consult school library media specialist"). If an item in the list is not appropriate for your assignment or project, do not place any number beside it.

_____ Consult school library media specialist

_____ Contact a digital reference service

_____ World Wide Web (See 3. Location & Access)

_____ Write to an electronic discussion group

_____ Books

_____ Periodicals

_____ Reference sources: encyclopedia, almanac, and atlas

_____ People in the community

_____ _____

_____ _____

_____ _____

_____ _____

3. **Big6 Step 3—Location & Access:** *Where can I find the sources and the information within the sources?*
    a. Search for non-Internet sources.
        Ask a library media specialist or librarian for assistance.
    b. Search the Internet.
        Start here if you need to search for a Web site. This guide will help you find Internet resources using search tools. Repeat steps as needed. Record answers and notes on this worksheet or a separate sheet of paper.

First search:

Search engine (name and address):_____

Search term: _____

Number of hits: _____ Need to refine search term? ☐ Yes ☐ No

Second search:

Search engine (name and address):_____

Search term: _____

Number of hits: _____ Need to refine search term? ☐ Yes ☐ No

Third search:

Search engine (name and address):_____

Search term: _____

Number of hits: _____ Need to refine search term? ☐ Yes ☐ No

Repeat process with other search engines/indexes if necessary. Read directions before using an unfamiliar search tool. (See Appendix B: Searching the Internet):

- Alta Vista <*http://www.altavista.com*>
- Yahoo <*http://www.yahoo.com*>
- Yahooligans <*http://www.yahooligans.com/*>
- HotBot <*http://www.hotbot.com/index.html*>
- WebCrawler <*http://www.webcrawler.com/*>
- Lycos <*http://www.lycos.com/*>
- Infoseek <*http://guide.infoseek.com/*>
- Excite <*http://www.excite.com/*>

c. Locate recommended or favorite sites (bookmarks)

d. List sites for further research

Web Site Name	Address (URL)

e. Communicate with:
- ☐ Experts
- ☐ Electronic discussion list
- ☐ Teacher
- ☐ Other: _____

4. **Big6 Step 4—Use of Information:** *How can I capture the information from the sources and decide which information is most important?*

a. Change format of Internet-based resources:
- ☐ Print
- ☐ Copy and paste into word processing file
- ☐ Download (save as file to disk)

b. Interact:
- ☐ Read
- ☐ View
- ☐ Listen

c. Extract information:
- ☐ Highlight
- ☐ Write notes on document, piece of paper or word processing file

d. Record citation information (See Appendix F: Citing Internet Sources) (Information below is adapted from Nueva Library Research Goal *http://www.nueva.pvt.k12.ca.us/~debbie/library/research/cit/mla/citwww1.html*)

For each Web site citation, record the following information:

Author (last name, first name): _____

Title of Web page: _____

Title of complete work: _____

Date created or last revised: _____

Full address (URL): _____

Date you saw it: _____

For each e-mail message citation, record the following information:

Author of message (last, first): _____

Author's e-mail address: _____

Subject (from "subject" line): _____

Date it was written: _____

Form of communication (personal e-mail or distribution list):

_____

5. **Big6 Step 5—Synthesis:** *How can I organize the information and present the results?*
   Organize the information:
   - ☐ Create outline
   - ☐ Write rough draft
   - ☐ Develop an argument in my own words

   Present:
   - ☐ Share: E-mail final product to class
   - ☐ Create: Report, Web page, poster, etc.
   - ☐ Practice presentation
   - ☐ Other: _____

6. **Big6 Step 6—Evaluation:** *How well did I do, and how can I do it better next time? Answer all questions that apply to this activity.*

   Task Definition
   How well did you:
   - ■ Understand the assignment?
   - ■ Focus your assignment topic?

   Information Seeking Strategies
   How well did you choose the best resources to help you with your assignment?

   Location & Access
   How well did you find the resources you were looking for?
   When searching the Internet:
   - ■ Which search engines worked best?
   - ■ Which search terms worked best?
   How well did you find the information you were looking for within the sources?

   Use of Information
   Which strategies worked best for using the information found on the Web—downloading, printing, note taking, etc.?
   Did you cite your sources accurately?

   Synthesis
   Did your final project meet the requirements of the assignment?
   Did it come out the way you wanted it to?

   General
   Did you encounter any problems during this activity? Please explain.
   How would you improve next time?

Coaching Students on the Internet
Using the Big6™

Worksheet 2[6]
Sample Completed Worksheet

Topic: <u>Egyptian Games</u>
Subject: <u>Social Studies</u>
Grade: <u>6</u>

1. **Big6 Step 1—Task Definition:** *What is the assignment? What is my topic?*

   How to Find Out
   Contact teacher or classmates to **clarify an assignment or discuss topics** by:
   - ☐ E-mail
   - ☐ Phone
   - ☑ In-person discussion
   - ☐ Videoconference
   - ☑ Online chat

   Notes: <u>The student started "chatting" with her teacher after school using special communications software available at school (the student accessed the software through a computer in the library media center and the teacher used a computer in her classroom). The student experienced some difficulties with the software, and decided it would be easier to walk to the classroom and talk to the teacher in person.</u>

   Find information to help **narrow or expand an assignment topic** in:
   - ☑ World Wide Web
   - ☐ Journal articles
   - ☐ Books (library catalog)
   - ☐ Messages to experts
   - ☐ Other sources

   Create your plan by completing the statements below:
   Original assignment: <u>Original assignment: To research an aspect of ancient Egyptian culture and present results as a final project in a format of the student's choice.</u>

   Date started: <u>3/15/99</u>   Date due: <u>5/1/99</u>

---

6 Based on Eisenberg, Michael B. and Berkowitz, Robert E. (1996). Helping with Homework: A Parent's Guide to Information Problem Solving. Syracuse, NY: ERIC Clearinghouse on Information and Technology, Syracuse University.

Research question/topic **ideas** (can brainstorm on separate sheet):
<u>Egyptian games-Hounds and Jackals</u>
<u>How old is the game?</u>
<u>Who played the game?</u>
<u>How do you play the game?</u>
<u>What did the original game board look like?</u>

Refined question/topic: <u>Research the Egyptian game, Hounds and Jackals.</u>
<u>Present results in a final report and instructional video that</u>
<u>will explain how to play the game.</u>

Types of information needed (check all that apply):
- ☑ Facts
- ☐ Opinion
- ☐ Numerical information
- ☐ Other: _____

Format of final product:
- ☑ Report
- ☐ Poster
- ☐ Computer-based presentation
- ☑ Video
- ☐ Web page
- ☐ Brochure/pamphlet
- ☐ Other: _____

2. **Big6 Step 2—Information Seeking Strategies:** *What sources should I use? Which sources are the best?*
   Review the list below and add any resources that you think would help with your assignment or question. Next, place numbers to the left of each item to indicate which ones are most likely to help you, in order of priority (for instance, if you think you should talk to your school library media specialist first, place a "1" to the left of "consult school library media specialist"). If an item in the list is not appropriate for your assignment or project, do not place any number beside it.

   _____ Consult school library media specialist

   _____ Contact a digital reference service

   __1__ World Wide Web (See 3. Location & Access)

   _____ Write to an electronic discussion group

   __2__ Books

   _____ Periodicals

   __3__ Reference sources: encyclopedia, almanac, and atlas

   _____ People in the community

   _____ _____

   _____ _____

   _____ _____

3. **Big6 Step 3—Location & Access:** *Where can I find the sources and the information within the sources?*
   a. Search for non-Internet sources.
      Ask a library media specialist or librarian for assistance.
   b. Search the Internet.
      Start here if you need to search for a Web site. This guide will help you find Internet resources using search tools. Repeat steps as needed. Record answers and notes on this worksheet or a separate sheet of paper.

First search:

Search engine (name and address): <u>AltaVista <www.altavista.com></u>

Search term: <u>"ancient Egypt"</u>

Number of hits: <u>37,857</u>   Need to refine search term?   ☑ Yes   ☐ No

Second search:

Search engine (name and address): <u>AltaVista</u>

Search term: <u>+"ancient Egypt" +games</u>

Number of hits: <u>26,125</u>   Need to refine search term?   ☑ Yes   ☐ No

Third search:

Search engine (name and address): <u>AltaVista</u>

Search term: <u>+"ancient Egypt" +games +"hounds and jackals"</u>

Number of hits: <u>36</u>   Need to refine search term?   ☐ Yes   ☑ No

Repeat process with other search engines/indexes if necessary. Read directions before using an unfamiliar search tool. (See Appendix B: Searching the Internet):
- Alta Vista <*http://www.altavista.com*>
- Yahoo <*http://www.yahoo.com*>
- Yahooligans <*http://www.yahooligans.com/*>
- HotBot <*http://www.hotbot.com/index.html*>
- WebCrawler <*http://www.webcrawler.com/*>
- Lycos <*http://www.lycos.com/*>
- Infoseek <*http://guide.infoseek.com/*>
- Excite <*http://www.excite.com/*>

   c. Locate recommended or favorite sites (bookmarks)

d. List sites for further research

Web Site Name	Address (URL)
"Dogs and Jackals" from "The Game Cabinet," an online games magazine	http://www.gamecabinet.com/history/DogsAndJackals.html

Notes: This was the only site in the search results that the student found helpful for her project. Most of the sites only mentioned the Hounds and Jackals (or "Dogs and Jackals") game in context of other games, or were commercial sites advertising games for sale.

e. Communicate with:
☐ Experts
☐ Electronic discussion list
☐ Teacher
☐ Other: _____

4. **Big6 Step 4—Use of Information:** *How can I capture the information from the sources and decide which information is most important?*

a. Change format of Internet-based resources:
☑ Print
☐ Copy and paste into word processing file
✳ Download (save as file to disk)
*Note: The student was interested in downloading an electronic version of the game that she found on the Web site. Unfortunately, in order to play the game, the student would need a special kind of software that wasn't available on her school computer.

b. Interact:
☑ Read
☑ View
☐ Listen

c. Extract information:
☑ Highlight
☑ Write notes on document, piece of paper or word processing file

d. Record citation information (See Appendix F: Citing Internet Sources). (The information below is adapted from Nueva Library Help: MLA Bibliographic Format— MLA Citing a Professional Web Page *http://www.nueva.pvt.k12.ca.us/~debbie/library/research/cit/mla/citwww1.html*)

For each Web site citation, record the following information:

Author (last name, first name): <u>Soubeyrand, Catherine</u>

Title of Web page: <u>Dogs and Jackals</u>

Title of complete work: <u>The Game Cabinet</u>

Date created or last revised: <u>26 Oct. 1998</u>

Full address (URL): <u>http://www.gamecabinet.com/history/</u>

<u>DogsAndJackals.html</u>

Date you saw it: <u>15 Mar. 1999</u>

For each e-mail message citation, record the following information:

Author of message (last, first): _____

Author's e-mail address: _____

Subject (from "subject" line): _____

Date it was written: _____

Form of communication (personal e-mail or distribution list):

_____

5. **Big6 Step 5—Synthesis:** *How can I organize the information and present the results?*
Organize the information:
☑ Create outline
☑ Write rough draft
☑ Develop an argument in my own words
Note: <u>The student organized the information for her report and video into three different categories: history of the game, how to play the game, and facts about the game.</u>

Present:
☐ Share: E-mail final product to class
☑ Create: Report, Web page, poster, etc.
☑ Practice presentation
☑ Other: <u>Shoot video with parent's help</u>

6. **Big6 Step 6—Evaluation:** *How well did I do, and how can I do it better next time? Answer all questions that apply to this activity.*

Task Definition

How well did you:

■ Understand the assignment? <u>I didn't understand the assignment very well at first. I wasn't sure what the teacher expected me to do until I talked to her about it.</u>

■ Focus your assignment topic? <u>I knew I wanted to concentrate on Hounds and Jackals since I first read about it.</u>

Information Seeking Strategies

How well did you choose the best resources to help you with your assignment? <u>I'm glad I chose books and the encyclopedia to find information about the game, because there were not many Web sites with good explanations.</u>

Location & Access

How well did you find the resources you were looking for? <u>It took me a few tries to get a good Internet search. I kept getting too many results until I used more search terms.</u>

When searching the Internet:
■ Which search engines worked best?
■ Which search terms worked best? <u>It worked best when I used more terms. The best search string was: +"ancient Egypt" +games +"hounds and jackals"</u>

How well did you find the information you were looking for within the sources? <u>It wasn't too hard to find the information I needed in the Web page, book and encyclopedia I used.</u>

Use of Information

Which strategies worked best for using the information found on the Web— downloading, printing, note-taking, etc.? <u>I printed out the Web site and highlighted the important things.</u>

Did you cite your sources properly? <u>Yes, I included everything in the bibliography.</u>

Synthesis

Did your final project meet the requirements of the assignment? <u>Yes</u>

Did it come out the way you wanted it to? <u>Yes and no. I didn't end up making the video, because I ran out of time and wanted to make sure I spent enough time on my report.</u>

General

Did you encounter any problems during this activity? Please explain. <u>Yes, I had one main problem. I could not find a lot of information on the game. If I had done a report on Egyptian games in general, I would have found more information on the subject.</u>

How would you improve next time? <u>I would do a project on a more common subject so I could find more information.</u>

Chapter Summary

- Information mentors can help students use the Internet within an information problem-solving process.
- Teachers, library media specialists, and other school staff can help students browse and search the Web, use e-mail, develop Web pages, and perform other Internet-related tasks. Parents can help students use the Internet at home and other locations.
- It is important to provide Internet access to students outside of school (e.g., home, public library).
- Parents most often help students use the Internet during Big6 steps 3: Location & Access; 4: Use of Information; and 5: Synthesis.
- Consider the following issues when using the Internet with K-12 students:
  - Provide access
  - Online safety
  - Quality of Internet materials
  - Copyright
  - Information mentor proficiency
- Information mentors can use the Big6 to guide students through Internet use for a given assignment or other information problem.

Chapter Pathfinder

Chapter 2—Coaching K-12 Students with the Internet

Internet Resources

Research and Web Citations from Nueva School
http://www.nueva.pvt.k12.ca.us/~debbie/library/research/research.html
This site is designed to help K-12 students develop research and information literacy skills. Guidance is offered on citing electronic and print sources using the MLA format. The site also includes tips on conducting research and special bibliographies on various topics.

Teacher Pathfinder Parent Building
http://teacherpathfinder.org/Parent/parent.html
As part of Teacher/Pathfinder's "educational Internet village," the "Parent Building" is designed to connect parents and children to family-friendly Internet sites. Links are provided to resources on several topics, including health, parenting, home schooling, preschool, involving the family in education, and fun for kids.

700+ Amazing, Spectacular, Mysterious, Wonderful Web Sites for Kids and the Adults Who Care About Them
http://www.ala.org/parentspage/greatsites/
A categorized list of sites compiled by the Children and Technology Committee of the Association for Library Service to Children, a division of the American Library Association.

ERIC Citations

ACCESS ERIC. (1997). *Parents guide to the Internet*. Rockville, MD: ACCESS ERIC, 26pp. (ED 410 952). The Internet is a vast network of computers that connects people and information all over the world. Children often know far more about computers than their parents do. However, children need their parents' involvement, experience, and judgment, whether the children are experienced computer users or just getting started. This booklet provides parents with basic information about how to use the computer to find information and communicate with others. It describes what is needed to get started on the Internet and points to some of the many interesting, helpful, and fun resources available online for parents and children. The book discusses: benefits of getting on the information superhighway; computer hardware and software basics; choosing an Internet service provider or online service; basics for exploring the World Wide Web and communicating with others on the Internet; tips for safe Internet use—to ensure that children have safe, productive, and enjoyable experiences on the Internet; encouraging information literacy; supporting school use of technology; and sample Internet sites. A glossary of computer and Internet terms is provided.

Anderson, C., (Ed.). (1996). CompuKids, 1996. *CompuKids, 2*(1-6). 49pp. (ED 405 953). This document consists of the 1996 issues of *CompuKids*, a bimonthly publication designed to assist children and their parents and teachers in getting the most out of using computers. The publication includes descriptions of available software, tips on hardware, and adaptations for Macintosh and IBM/Windows products. Regular features include: (1) "For Kids by KIDS," displaying children's computer products and stories; (2) "I Need Help!" which lists available software for particular activities, required computer configurations, the company publishing the software, and recommended ages. Included in this volume are articles on using computers in play, literacy/reading and computers, the Internet, keyboarding, word processing, creative writing software, stages of children's writing, summer activities, adaptive software programs to make accessing a computer easier for children, and innovative ways that computers can be used by children with disabilities.

Berkowitz, R. (1998). Helping with homework: A parent's guide to information problem-solving. *Emergency Librarian, 25*(4), 45-46. (EJ 565 458). Summarizes the Big6 Skills information problem-solving approach: (1) Task Definition; (2) Information Seeking Strategies; (3) Location and Access; (4) Use of Information; (5) Synthesis; and (6) Evaluation. Discusses parent and student roles in information problem solving, the value of assignments, and technology and the Big6.

Direct Marketing Association. (1997). *Get cyber savvy: A family guide. The DMA's guide to parenting skills for the digital age: Online basics, behavior and privacy*. NY: Direct Marketing Association, 28pp. (ED 414 051). The ability to meet people, visit places around the globe, and make purchases online has added a new dimension to teaching children about the opportunities and accompanying risks that exist in everyday life. The Direct Marketing Association has created this guide to information use, behavior, and privacy on the Internet to help parents supervise their children's learning experiences, even for parents who do not understand the technology well enough to oversee their children's online use. Areas addressed include: (1) how common sense applies to the Internet, easy-to-use parental control technologies, and what the Internet offers; (2) a short quiz to see how much parents already know about the Internet and to get them prepared for other activities; (3) a guided tour, including e-mail, Listservs, World Wide Web, uniform resource locators, and encryption, for parents to follow in the workbook or online at the computer; (4) sample cases of real situations parents and children may encounter online, including issues of personal information, surveys, Web stores, password, and directories, and the opportunity to discuss them; and (5) how to develop a set of rules and guidelines for enjoying cyberspace in families, which includes a family pledge document for each family member to sign.

Eisenberg, M. (1997). Helping with homework. *Big6 Newsletter, 1*(1), 4-5. (EJ 562 882). Discussion of the parents' role in homework highlights use of the Big6 Skills to focus on information literacy and information problem-solving processes rather than focusing on having parents help with the actual subject area content. The emphasis is on having parents act as guides and helpers rather than as teachers.

Eisenberg, M. B., & Berkowitz, R. E. (1996). *Helping with homework: A parent's guide to information problem-solving*. Syracuse, NY: ERIC Clearinghouse on Information and Technology. (ED 418 699). The purpose of this book is to help parents become partners in their children's success in school by offering them practical ways to help with homework and assignments. Parents can use the Big Six Skills information problem-solving process to effectively deal with the abundance of information available from many sources and guide their children through school assignments. The Big Six Skills apply to any problem or activity that requires a solution or result based on information: task definition, information seeking strategies, location and access, use of information, synthesis, and evaluation. There are six chapters in the book: (1) "The Big Six Approach: A Framework for Helping Children"; (2) "What Your Children Face Every Day in School: Assignments"; (3) "The Big Six Applied: A Framework for Helping Children with Homework"; (4) "Computers, the Internet, and Other Technologies: Can They Really Make a Difference?"; (5) "Assisting with Assignments: Examples from Various Subjects"; and (6) "Bringing It All Together: A Parent Conversation with Mike and Bob." Appendices include the Big Six Assignment Organizer, applying the Big Six to sample homework assignments, Big Six Skills overhead transparency masters and bookmark, background information on the Educational Resources Information Center (ERIC), and a selected bibliography of ERIC documents.

Eisenberg, M. B., & Berkowitz, R. E. (1996). Helping with homework: A parent's guide to information problem-solving. *ERIC Digest*. Syracuse, NY: ERIC Clearinghouse on Information and Technology. (ED 402 950).
http://www.ed.gov/databases/ERIC_Digests/ed402950.html
Parents can play an important role in helping their children succeed in school. This ERIC Digest presents the Big Six Skills problem-solving method as an effective approach for parents. The Big Six Skills apply to any problem or activity that requires a solution or result based on information. The Big Six can help parents effectively deal with the abundance of information available from many sources to guide their children through school assignments. The Big Six consists of: task definition, information seeking strategies, location and access, use of information, synthesis, and evaluation. In this approach, the parent assumes the role of a "coach" while the child assumes the role of a "thinker and doer." The parent guides the student through all the steps it takes to complete the assignment, while the child thinks about what he or she needs to do at each step and then finds appropriate ways to do it. The Big Six approach recognizes the benefits of technology such as computers, e-mail, and the Internet for organizing information and for access to non-traditional sources of information. The Big Six approach can help parents effectively guide their children through assignments and at the same time help their children become independent learners and users of information. (Contains 10 references.)

Lazarus, W., & Lipper, L. (1996). *The parents' guide to the information superhighway: rules and tools for families online.* Santa Monica, CA: Children's Partnership, 37pp. (ED 401 872). Computers and online services are becoming a part of children's lives. This guide is designed to introduce parents to the information superhighway and to parenting in a world of computers and new forms of media. Prepared by the Children's Partnership, with assistance from the National PTA and the National Urban League, this guide provides tools and rules for parents to use with children at home, at school, and in the community. The guide helps parents gain an understanding of the technology, learn what is at stake for them and their children, and how they can help their children reap the benefits of the information age. The following sections are included: (1) "What is the Information Superhighway?"; (2) "What's at Stake—Why Computers Matter to Your Child"; (3) "What Does Using Computers Actually Do for Your Child?"; (4) "When Is Your Child Ready?"; (5) "Have We Been Here Before?"; (6) "Some Basic Rules"; (7) "Setting Up To Go Online"; (8) "Alternatives to a Home Computer"; (9) "How Can You Find Good Places To Go and Things To Do Online?"; (10) "How Can You Keep Your Child Safe Online?"; (11) "At School—Getting Involved with Technology"; and (12) "Helping Ensure that All Children Have an On-Ramp." Includes appendices with resources for further help and a glossary.

Magid, L. J. (1996). Protecting your child on the information highway: What parents need to know. *Montessori-Life,* (8)1, 26. (EJ 520 499). Discusses how parents can reduce the risks of inappropriate Internet use and ensure positive online experiences for their children. Gives guidelines for family rules and personal rules that each young user should know and understand.

Marsh, M., & Alden, S. B., (Ed.). (1995). *Everything you need to know (but were afraid to ask kids) about the information highway (including some suggestions & ideas that your children may not even know—yet!).* Palo Alto, CA: Computer Learning Foundation, 102pp. (ED 401 873). The information highway is an exciting place for children and families to visit, explore, and learn about together. This book teaches parents basic knowledge about the information highway and how to use it with children. The following topics are covered in this book: (1) What is the Information Highway? (2) What is Telecommunications?; (3) Why You & Your Children Want To Telecommunicate; (4) Getting Connected; (5) Guidelines for Making Sure that Everything Works with Everything Else; (6) Sending and Receiving Information through Your Computer; (7) Introducing Yourself & Your Children; (8) Ten Terrific Telecommunications Tips; (9) How Safe Is it Online for Children?; (10) Differences in Supervision and Safety of Online Services; (11) eWorld's Rules for Living in an Electronic World; (12) My Rules for Online Safety; (13) Setting Your Standards & Ground Rules for Safe, Legal, and Efficient Online Use; (14) Online Manners (Netiquette) for Students; (15) Kids Only Online (KOOL) Rules from America Online; (16) Money-Saving Suggestions; (17) Computer Learning Foundation Code of Responsible Computing; (18) The Internet; (19) Commercial Online Services; (20) Bulletin Board Systems (BBS); (21) Universal Truths; (22) Working with Your Children; (23) Using Telecommunications with Children Experiencing Peer Problems or with Disabilities; (24) Activities for Preschool Children; (25) Activities for Ages Six to Eight; (26) Activities for Ages Nine to Twelve; (27) Ages Thirteen to Eighteen and Beyond; (28) Family Activities; (29) Activating the Home-School Connection; and (30) Closing Thoughts: The Future. Contains a list of resources, contacts, a glossary of terms, and an index.

Right and wrong online. Teaching your children ethics in cyberspace. (1998). *Our-Children*, (23)4, 32-33. (EJ 558 963). Parents must describe and reinforce the importance of truthfulness, responsibility, and respect when their children use the Internet. The paper presents potential situations that could arise and discusses issues related to the law online, copyrighted materials, copying or distributing software, privacy, hacking, and obscenity. A sidebar offers tips to keep children safe online.

Communicating with Students on the Internet

Communicating with Students on the Internet

Chapter Profile

This chapter is designed to help information mentors communicate with and provide information for K-12 students online. It provides background on the role of telecommunications activities in education, particularly Ask-an-Expert services and telementoring projects, and offers suggestions to information mentors for promoting the use of information problem-solving through online communications. Suggestions are also included to help educators manage successful telecommunications activities in their classrooms.

Communicate effectively with students via the Internet to provide guidance in information problem-solving, subject areas, and personal development.

Before reading this chapter, you should be able to:
1. Use e-mail or Web-based communications tools.

This chapter will prepare you to:
1. Understand advantages of telecommunications activities in K-12 education.
2. Identify different types of instructional opportunities involving communication between students and subject or process experts.
3. Describe differences between AskA services and telementoring programs, including the various roles of experts in AskA services and telementoring programs.
4. Identify issues in communicating with students online.
5. Identify issues in participating in telecommunications activities from a classroom perspective.
6. Promote the Big6 in online communications with students.

Online Communication and Learning

The Internet has added a new dimension to the ways that we communicate with each other. Students can "chat" with teachers to clarify an assignment; e-mail students in other countries; and ask questions of scientists, mathematicians, and other experts via the Web. Students from anywhere in the world can communicate with a classroom in Milan, volcanologists in Hawaii, NASA Space Shuttle Engineers, Asian studies experts, or meteorologists in the Antarctic.

Telecommunications activities that place students in contact with adult experts can be very motivating for students. Students can communicate and build relationships with adults who are "passionate about a topic," and they can pursue academic topics of interest in a private environment without being criticized by their peers (Harris, 1999, phone conversation). Such activities are especially appropriate for middle school students (grades 5-8 in the United States), because such activities support both curriculum requirements and developmental needs including (Yee, 1998, par. 15):

- Development of research skills
- Publishing and sharing student work
- Immediacy and spontaneity of communication, and
- Understanding cultural and political diversity.

Telecommunication Opportunities

There are several types of telecommunications activities that can be used in instruction. Communication can occur _synchronously_ (i.e., in real-time), such as Internet Relay Chat and audio or video conferencing, or _asynchronously_, such as e-mail and electronic discussion groups. Harris (1998) identifies three types of activities that foster telecollaboration (collaboration with distant colleagues) and teleresearch (research using resources located elsewhere) (p. 17):

- Interpersonal exchange—activities where students communicate electronically with others (e.g., keypals, ask-an-expert services, etc.) (p. 18)
- Information collection and analysis—activities involving "collecting, compiling, and comparing" information with others (p. 33)
- Problem solving—activities in which students communicate with others to achieve a specific goal (e.g., solve problems or answer questions based on clues, provide feedback to other students based on written work, or develop a common written product) (p. 40).

This chapter focuses on activities involving interpersonal exchange, specifically telementoring and question-and-answer activities that place students in contact with subject matter, information referral, and instructional experts. The suggestions made in this chapter are intended to help such experts communicate effectively with students using the Big6 process.

AskA Services and Telementoring Activities

Although question-and-answer services (known as AskA services) and telementoring programs both place students in touch with experts, the two activities differ in many ways, including the purpose of communication, length of time commitment, and the nature of messages exchanged.

AskA services, named for such services as "Ask A Scientist" and "Ask A Librarian," are Internet-based question/answer and referral services that can assist students (as well as the general public) in answering questions. AskA services are also referred to as *digital reference* services, because they fulfill a role similar to reference services in the library and information professions. In fact, many digital reference services are operated by information professionals who match people to resources or to direct knowledge to satisfy specific information needs. Some digital reference services help K-12 students with school-related questions (e.g., KidsConnect); some are designed for K-12 researchers and educators (e.g., AskERIC); and other services offer specific subject expertise to K-12 students and others (e.g., MAD Scientist Network, Ask Dr. Math). Current digital reference services offer two main types of expertise-subject matter (providing mostly factual information) and process (providing mostly resource referral and instruction).

Examples of AskA services for K-12 students, educators and parents are collected and catalogued at the Virtual Reference Desk's AskA+ Locator *(http://www.vrd.org/locator/subject.html)*. Some exemplary AskA services include[7]:

- *AskERIC* is a personalized AskA service providing education information to teachers, librarians, counselors, administrators, parents, and others. It began in 1992 as a project of the ERIC Clearinghouse on Information & Technology at Syracuse University. Today, it encompasses the resources of the entire ERIC system and beyond. *http://www.askeric.org/*

- *KidsConnect* is a question answering, help, and referral service for K-12 students on the Internet. The goal of the service is to help students access and use the information available on the Internet effectively and efficiently. KidsConnect is a component of ICONnect, a technology initiative of the American Association of School Librarians (AASL), a division of the American Library Association. *http://www.ala.org/ICONN/AskKC.html*

- *How Things Work*, founded and operated by a physics professor at the University of Virginia, is a question-and-answer service for users of all ages with any kind of physics question. The site also features a searchable index of previously answered questions, a recent questions list, and links to other related resources. *http://landau1.phys.virginia.edu/Education/Teaching/HowThingsWork/home.html*

- *MAD Scientist Network* is composed of over 500 scientists from around the world. The network answers questions in many areas of science and includes an online archive of question-answer sets in addition to other resources. The MAD Scientist Network is operated by Washington University School of Medicine, St. Louis; funding sources include the Howard Hughes Medical Institute and the Washington University School of Medicine Alumni Association. *http://madsci.wustl.edu/*

- *Ask Dr. Math* is a question-and-answer service for K-12 math teachers and students. The service provides an archive that is searchable by grade level and topic and includes such features as frequently asked questions (FAQ), archives, and other resources. Ask Dr. Math is a service of the Math Forum. *http://mathforum.com/dr.math/*

---

7   For more information on AskA services for K-12 education, see Kasowitz, 1999.

- *Ask Shamu* is a question-and-answer service of Sea World, Inc. and Busch Entertainment Corp. Ask Shamu answers questions about the ocean and marine animals. Ask Shamu answers 100% of the questions received, and answers are short and factual with minimal references. A toll-free number (1-800-23SHAMU) is provided for students to submit questions by telephone and for teachers to request curriculum materials. The site also features a FAQ, curriculum guides, and more.
  http://www.seaworld.org/ask_shamu/asintro.html
- *Ask Joan of Art* is an AskA service of the National Museum of American Art of the Smithsonian Institution. Information specialists at the museum answer questions regarding American art. Specific questions receive brief, factual responses, while users with broad queries are directed to sources to aid in their research.
  http://www.nmaa.si.edu/referencedesk/

Telementoring activities involve matching students or classrooms with subject experts for an extended period of time; experts can guide students toward achieving a curriculum-related goal or simply participate in conversations about a specific topic or career. Subject expert telementors serve as "knowledge apprentices" who address higher-level comprehension skills rather than one-time explanation or information referral (Harris, 1999, phone conversation). Telementoring exchanges can be formal or informal, but to be effective, telementoring programs should "build online conversation spaces, activities, support, and facilitation" (Bennett, 1997, p. 50).

Examples of telementoring projects include:

- *Telementoring Young Women in Science, Engineering, and Computing* (*http://www.edc.org/CCT/telementoring*)—Funded by the National Science Foundation, this project links role models to high school students pursuing scientific and technical fields. Telementoring relationships last for one year and concentrate on career guidance and personal development. The project is run by the Education Development Center's Center for Children and Technology (Bennett, 1997).
- *Electronic Emissary Project (http://www.tapr.org/emissary)*—This project maintains a database of mentors in many different areas of subject expertise and matches students and teachers to experts in a specific curriculum topic. Mentor to classroom communications are facilitated by Electronic Emissary staff members who have expertise in instruction and online projects (Harris, 1998). The project is coordinated from the University of Texas at Austin and receives support from the Texas Center for Educational Technology (TCET) and the University of Texas at Austin's College of Education (Electronic Emissary, 1998).
- *International Telementor Center (http://www.telementor.org)*—This program, at the Center for Science, Mathematics & Technology Education at the Colorado State University (CSMATE), facilitates telementoring relationships between professionals and students worldwide. Its best-known program is the HP Telementor Program that places Hewlett-Packard employees in contact with students. Its goal is to encourage students to excel in science and math and to actively pursue academic areas of interest in an enjoyable way (International Telementor Center, 1999).

Information Mentor Spotlight—Online Experts

Experts in Telecommunications Activities

Experts who communicate with students as part of telementoring or question-and-answer activities can be information mentors. While some experts guide students through parts of or the whole information problem-solving process, others simply serve as information resources themselves. Whatever the case, all experts may consider the information problem-solving process in communicating with students as a way to help students place the communication exchange (or series of exchanges) in perspective with the greater curriculum-related goal or objective. In addition, experts can rely on an information problem-solving model while preparing and framing their own communications to students.

Although it takes a variety of individuals and job functions to make an AskA service or telementoring program function successfully, the experts who interact directly with K-12 students often fall into the following categories:

AskA Service

■ **Subject experts.** These experts can range from NASA space scientists to Canadian geography experts to *New York Times* reporters who answer questions based on their own subject expertise and occasionally related information resources.

■ **Information specialists.** These include school, public, and special librarians, and other information professionals who are skilled in pointing people to information in general or in a specific discipline (e.g., art, education, etc.). Information specialists frequently guide students and other "questioners" through the steps to find needed information.

Telementoring Program

■ **Subject area telementors.** Their range of expertise can be as varied as AskA service subject experts, but their responsibilities are different. They must commit to a particular student or class for a longer time period and must be able to develop a relationship through online exchanges.

■ **Telementoring facilitators.** Some telementoring programs offer mediation between K-12 school participants and subject area telementors in order to "build mutually accessible bridges between their differing workplaces" (Harris, 1996, 54). For instance, facilitators of the Electronic Emissary project, who have expertise in Internet-based communication as well as education, monitor the entire telementoring experience in order to provide suggestions and resources and check for student understanding of telementors' explanations (Harris, 1999 phone call). Telementoring programs that do not utilize the facilitator role often provide training programs to prepare subject area telementors to handle communications on their own (Bennett, 1997).

Considerations for Online Communications

Online experts in all contexts should be aware of certain issues when communicating with K-12 students. It is important for educators, parents, and other information mentors to consider these issues as well.

Issues for Online Experts

- **Purpose of communication.** The purpose of communication between an expert and a student is defined by the nature of the program. For instance, AskA service experts are usually responsible for providing factual explanations or information referral for academic projects or personal interests; and telementor subject experts are sometimes responsible for providing factual explanations as well as providing encouragement to students to pursue their interests. (Responsibilities are normally presented to experts during training.) In addition to these general roles, experts can determine the purpose of a specific communication experience or relationship through a student's question to an AskA service or a teacher's lesson plan submission or project description to a telementoring program.

- **Age-appropriate communication**. One of the advantages of communicating with an online expert is that information may be tailored to the specific needs, skill levels, and interests of a particular student. Subject area experts who commonly use technical vocabulary and terms with adult colleagues sometimes find it difficult to phrase their communications in language that K-12 students can understand. This is less of a problem for AskA services and telementoring programs that rely on facilitators or moderators to review and interpret messages; but experts who communicate directly with children should pay careful attention to the language and tone used. Experts should make sure their messages are free of undefined jargon, acronyms, or abbreviations. Experts should also refer students to resources that are appropriate for their age and experience levels.

- **Clear communication and presentation**. It is often more difficult to express oneself using e-mail than it is face-to-face or over the phone. Writing clearly helps to get one's point across and can increase the value of the AskA or telementoring experience. Tips include (adapted from Ekhaml, 1996):
  a) Clear language—Make sure the message is written clearly. (If you received this message, would you find it easy to read?) Include important information at the beginning of the message (e.g., summary of the entire message).
  b) Correct grammar and spelling—Online experts can act as role models for proper language usage. Utilize spell-check software and dictionaries whenever necessary.
  c) Clear presentation—One way to enhance readability of your response is to leave plenty of white space between different ideas or recommended resources. Break long paragraphs into smaller ones, and separate different ideas from each other. For indentation of text, use tabs instead of spaces.
  d) Accessibility/ease of use—Avoid formatting styles that aren't readable across various e-mail programs. This includes bold, italic, underlined type, or bullets. One alternative is to use asterisks or dashes to separate text and to list items.

- **Privacy**. Most telementoring programs and AskA services should have policies about the privacy of communications between experts and students. Some services and programs make online exchanges available on their Web sites to share with site visitors or archive questions and answers to use for research. It is important wherever possible to remove any information from exchanges that could potentially identify a student, teacher, or a school, unless permission has been granted. (Teachers and students should be cautious of sharing any personal information online.)

- **Safety**. Whenever possible, use communications channels set up by the AskA service or telementoring program, or use your own personal e-mail account to communicate with students. Chat servers should be avoided for AskA and telementoring experiences involving K-12 students, because access to inappropriate materials often cannot be controlled in such environments (Wear, 1998).

- **Differences in context**. It is important for experts to understand the culture and context of the K-12 classroom (and vice versa). Many online experts work in offices where they have easy access to e-mail all day long. Students and teachers may only have the opportunity to communicate with an expert during certain times or on certain days of the week (Harris, 1996). (On the other hand, students and teachers should understand that experts are busy people who volunteer their free time to participate in the experience, and may not be able to correspond as often or as quickly as they would like.)

- **Frequency of communication**. Some programs and services have policies stating how often or how quickly an expert should communicate with a student. For instance, the HP Telementor Program advises its mentors to correspond with their proteges at least two to three times per week during the course of a commitment (International Telementor Center, 1999). According to an expert panel for K-12 AskA services, the "turnaround time" (the amount of time before a question is answered) should be two to five days[8]. Regardless of the frequency of communication, programs should set clear expectations for everyone involved in the experience.

Additional Issues for Educators and Others

- **Integration with curriculum**. Students and educators can communicate with online experts at different points during lessons or projects[9]. The telecommunications experience should supplement previously defined goals and objectives, rather than add new goals and objectives just for the sake of the experience. In addition, AskA services and telementors should not be used solely for e-mail or Internet practice (unless there has been some agreement otherwise), because most experts volunteer their time to share valuable information.

- **Preparation**. Teachers can help students plan ahead for a telecommunications experience by having them outline or compose messages in advance. Teachers can also ensure that students have the necessary technical capabilities to participate in telecommunications activities. This is especially important for telementoring activities where students are expected to communicate regularly with their mentor.

---

8   The Virtual Reference Desk expert panel for 1999, consisting of representatives from school, public, and academic libraries and digital reference services, discusses issues of quality criteria in digital reference services for K-12 education (see *http://www.vrd.org/panel/*).

9   See The Virtual Reference Desk Learning Center at: *http://www.vrd.org/k12/k-12home.html* for suggestions on using AskA services with K-12 students.

- **Alternative resources**. There are usually multiple ways to find information for a given question or topic. Don't forget to check the school library media center or public library; many answers can be found in encyclopedias, almanacs, and other print or electronic sources. Online experts should be consulted for information and guidance that is not available within the school or in other accessible resources.
- **Ongoing management**. Teachers should be involved throughout the whole communications process by monitoring student messages, keeping the pace of correspondence, and contacting experts or programs with questions and problems.
- **Express appreciation**. As previously mentioned, many experts are people who volunteer their time to share information and thoughts with students. While a large part of the reward comes from the experience itself, experts are always happy to know that their time and efforts are appreciated. For instance, teachers and students can send a "thank you" message to an AskA service expert upon receiving a response.

Information Problem-Solving in Online Communications

This section discusses the Big6 and other considerations that can enhance telecommunications transactions between experts and children. Using these guidelines, online experts can ensure effective communication and help children become better information users. Online experts can help students improve their overall information problem-solving skills by framing their responses in a Big6 context and helping students identify their place in the whole information problem-solving process. In addition, online experts can follow the Big6 process when composing their responses to include the most appropriate and accurate information to help students answer their own questions[10].

All messages submitted to digital reference services include at least one information problem or question. Messages exchanged during a telementoring project may or may not include a specific information problem. Some of the messages exchanged simply contain thoughts and feelings that are communicated as part of building the telementoring relationship. In many cases, however, the telementoring activities are a component of a larger curriculum unit or lesson that incorporates one or more information problems. Common types of information problems addressed in telementoring exchanges involve career exploration and personal decision-making as well as curriculum topics. While telementors should not be viewed as information sources for straight question-answering, some of the information that they provide can be used by students to make decisions during the information problem-solving process. For instance, encouraging and descriptive messages from an actor may help a high school student decide to pursue drama in college; or a chemist may help a middle school student decide to conduct a science fair project using a particular method.

Online experts can provide guidance to children in all steps of the Big6. By demonstrating their own use of the Big6, they provide models for students to follow. The following explanations and examples are designed to help online experts decide which areas are important to address in particular situations. Information is adapted from "Promoting Information Problem-Solving in Digital Reference Responses" (*http://www.vrd.org/training/ips.html*):

---

10 See *http://www.vrd.org/training/guide.htm* for guidelines to help AskA service experts compose responses using the Big6.

Step 1: Task Definition. As many online experts know, students are not always clear in communicating specific questions or problems. For instance, students may write to an AskA service with a question that is too narrowly focused or may indicate an ineffective research strategy. AskA service experts can provide tips and questions for students to think about to focus on a specific information problem. They may also refer students to other individuals who can help them with this process (e.g., teachers, parents).

Example: Question with Limited Information

To: Law Experts
Who was the woman who lobbied for the child safety restraint law?
From: Danielle

Hello,
Thank you for your question. In order to help you, I need a little more information. Do you happen to know what state the woman was from or what year the law was passed? Please write back and we'd be glad to help you with your research.
Thanks, M. Judge, Ask-A-Lawyer

Example: Question with Narrow Focus

To: Dr. Electric
Will it make sense to put solar panels around a ball field to save electricity?
From: Mark L.

Mark,
For a research question like this, you will need to go through a few different steps to find an answer. You will probably need to answer these questions: How many watts does it take to light up a stadium? Will this be an indoor or outdoor stadium? Will you need heat and air conditioning besides light energy? Before you do your research, it would be a good idea to brainstorm as many of these kinds of questions as possible....

In similar ways, telementors can help students identify their task in terms of a class project or their ultimate goal for the telementoring relationship. This task identification process may occur as a more casual conversation. In a telementoring situation, the student (or teacher) is usually responsible for presenting a task to the telementor program (such as a specific unit or lesson within the curriculum) and then the student and telementor collaborate to reach project goals.

The telementor can help narrow or expand a research focus by asking questions such as "Are you interested in x, y, or z?"

Example: Telementor Exchange to Identify Focus of Project[11]

Student: Hi, You probably already know that we're supposed to write a report about what jobs we want to have when we're adults. I'm having trouble deciding what to be. I'm interested in weather like thunderstorms and tornadoes and stuff. I also like music and animals.

Mentor: Hi Brian, Sounds like you've got a few different kinds of interests. That's great! What do you like about thunderstorms and other weather patterns? Do you think you would want to study weather changes and make predictions as to what the weather will do next? People who do that are called meteorologists....

---

11 This example is adapted from the "Exploring Your Interests" lesson in which HP Telementors helped students at McGraw Elementary School in Fort Collins, Colorado. (*http://www.telementor.org/hp/projects/capozza.html*).

Step 2: Information Seeking Strategies. After helping a student narrow his/her focus (either by providing suggestions or requesting additional information), an online expert can guide the student to information resources. This can include the expert's own knowledge, resources such as a Web site, book, or journal, or other individuals with the required knowledge. It is important to explain why certain information resources are better for a particular question than others. This will help students make their own decisions about resources for future information problems.

It is also a good idea to refer K-12 students to their library media specialists (LMS) in order to emphasize that their LMS are information experts in their schools who can guide them to local and remote resources. Students and educators should be aware that AskA services and telementors can supplement (not replace) the information resources and services available in schools.

Examples: Suggested Information Seeking Strategies from AskA Services

> …Although there are many Web sites about hurricanes, a simple article in a general or science encyclopedia will best answer your question: "How are hurricanes formed?" Ask your school library media specialist to guide you to an encyclopedia or to other resources on hurricanes in your school library media center.

> …The Web sites listed above contain information on basic parts of a book report. While these sites can give you some ideas, it is very important that you find out from your teacher what you are supposed to include in this particular assignment.

Examples: Suggested Information Seeking Strategies from Telementors[12]

> …If you're interested in learning about what news reporters do, maybe you can arrange to write an article for your school newspaper about being a reporter for a day, and then contact local news stations and newspapers to see if you can accompany a reporter for a day.

Step 3: Location & Access. AskA service experts and telementors can help students find sources and information that can help them answer a question or make a decision. Some AskA services may conduct an information search and then explain to the student the methods used. By describing the decisions they make in locating and accessing information, online experts can help teach students to search for information and use resources effectively on their own. This method can apply to information found in all types of resources, including Web search engines, indexes, or databases, but is especially important when referring students to Internet resources. Components used in these types of responses include:

- **Information path.** Describe the steps taken to find the source and to find relevant information within the source. For instance, if a search engine was used to look up Internet sites on a certain topic, include in the message the name and URL of the search engine and the search terms used. In addition, online experts should direct the student to the specific page(s) within a site or the specific area within a page (e.g., links, paragraphs, graphics) that most appropriately addresses the student's question.

---

12 This example is adapted from an exchange between a student at Lanier Middle School in Houston, TX, and a journalist from California (*http://www.rice.edu/armadillo/Schools/Lanier/EEP/97-98/freibero.html*) as part of an Electronic Emissary telementoring project.

- **Description of source**. In a response, it is helpful to include descriptions of each source listed. This includes the origin of information (e.g., the organization or individual responsible for the information on a Web site, author and/or publisher of book), content (i.e., the main focus), special features, and reason for selection (i.e., does the Web site address the student's question in a unique way?).
- **Citation information**. Whether the referred resources are on the Internet or in other formats, it is extremely important to include proper citation information in a response. An easy way to transfer citation information from the Internet to an e-mail message is to copy and paste relevant information, such as title, URL and author, if available. (See Appendix F for resources on citing electronic sources.)

AskA services may guide students to use all types of information resources such as encyclopedias, books, Web sites, and periodical databases.

Examples: AskA Services—Suggestions for Locating Information Resources

Internet Encyclopedia
…To find out what pigs eat, I went to an Internet encyclopedia called Encarta Online *http://encarta.msn.com/EncartaHome.asp*. You could also use a print or CD-ROM encyclopedia in your library or at home. In the search box, I typed "pigs." This brought me to a list of articles. I clicked on "pig" and then was brought to a page that said "see Hog." I clicked on "hog" (another word for pig) and got a whole page of information about the pig including what it eats.

Library Catalog
…To find a biography on a particular individual, look up the name, last name first. In our library, biographies are in "921," but in other libraries they could also be in "92," "B," or "BIO." (Ask your librarian to help you find the biography section of your library.) To find a biography on someone in a particular group or profession, look up such headings as:

> Presidents – United States – Biography
> Explorers – Great Britain – Biography
> Sports – United States – Biography

Web Site
…City.Net Peru *http://www.city.net/countries/peru/#cities*
At the bottom of the page, click on Lima, Miraflores, or Pacasmayo to find links to information on these three major cities in Peru. After clicking on a city name, scroll down the page to "travel and tourism" and pick a link for more detailed information on the cities.

For instance, go to the Internet address for City.Net Peru (written above) and click on "Lima" at the bottom of the page. On the next page, "City.Net Lima, Peru," scroll down to "travel and tourism" and then click on "Lima: A Quick Tour." This page will tell you about the history, population, climate and other details about Lima, the capital of Peru.

Telementors are more likely to discuss information searching with students as part of the telementoring experience. In addition to telementors suggesting resources to students, students may also share resource ideas with their telementors. This gives students and telementors an opportunity to discuss the types of information found in different types of resources as well as the methods used to find information.

Example: Telementoring Exchange Discussing Location of Information Resources

> *Mentor:* Did you try using the Alta Vista search engine for information about ethical issues in altering photos using digital technology? I just searched using the term: +digital +photograph +ethics and I found one site that I thought would be helpful: Issues and Ethics Involved in Photojournalism (*http://s9000.furman.edu/~eharmon/team2/issues.html*).
>
> *Student:* Thanks. That's a good site. I found this one searching WebCrawler: *http://metalab.unc.edu/nppa/epw/epw6/longethc.html*. My librarian is also helping me to use the periodical database to find magazine articles.

Step 4: Use of Information. AskA service experts and telementors can guide students in using information effectively. After suggesting an answer or a referral to additional resources, they can remind students of the various methods for using information: copying and pasting from the Internet to word processing programs, printing out information from the computer, taking notes, and highlighting important passages (Eisenberg & Johnson, 1996). In addition to suggesting methods for recording and highlighting information, it is also extremely important to remind students to cite their sources.

Example: Methods for Using Information

> …The "Children's Activities" Web page *http://www.history.org/places/geddy/geddychi.htm* from the "Colonial Williamsburg" Web site has lots of information that can answer your question "What did kids do during American Colonial times?" Print out the Web page or skim through it on the screen and take notes on the parts that answer your question best. A good set of notes will help you later to write your report in your own words.
>
> …Once you get to a Web site, you can use the source by reading it, looking at pictures, or listening to it if there is sound. If you are contacting an expert, you would use the source by listening to the person talk over the phone or by reading an e-mail message (like this one!). While you're listening, reading, looking, etc., you should take notes about what you learn.

Example: Methods for Citing Sources

Also, remember to cite the sources you use when you are writing your paper. To include Web pages in a bibliography you can follow this format:

[name of author]. ["Title of page"]. [Title of Source]. [year]. [Web address] [date you looked at it on the Web].

For example, the encyclopedia article I included would look like this:

"ghost." Britannica Online. 1998. <*http://www.eb.com:180/cgi-bin/g?DocF=micro/233/37.html*> [Accessed 11 March 1998].

(For additional information on citing Internet sources, see Appendix F.)

Step 5: Synthesis. This step helps students present information that they've gathered from various information sources. For AskA service experts, helping students synthesize information can be a bit tricky unless they know something about the intended final product. If the intended product is not known, AskA service experts can offer resources and tips as appropriate. Below are some examples for guiding students who are synthesizing information.

Example: Synthesis Help for a Long-term Assignment

…Once you have all the information you need—costs for owning each animal— you will need to put all the information together. The way you do this depends on your class assignment. It may be a report, chart, poster, etc.

During this step you will also be able to answer your question "Which is the worst pet?"

Example: Synthesis Help for a Math Problem Dealing with Order of Operations

…So, for your first question (a+1/2 > 4), since you don't have any parentheses or multiplication, you should start by trying to get the "a" by itself on the left side. That means you need to get the 1/2 on the right side. How can you take the 1/2 away from the left side? Subtract, right? Remember that in algebra, you need to do the same thing to both sides of the equation. So, you also need to subtract 1/2 from 4.

Your equation will look like this: a > 4 - 1/2

Now just do the subtraction. Remember to first find the lowest common denominator of 4/1 and 1/2!

During synthesis, telementors can help students in several ways. They can collaborate with students on different ways to present information, such as building a Web site (Neils, 1999, phone call), help students weigh pros and cons in decision-making, and guide students through revision processes to help students create quality products. Telementors can also go beyond the limits of classroom assignments and show how the information and knowledge can be applied in "real world" situations (Harris, 1999, phone call).

Example: Synthesis in a Telementoring Exchange

Mentor: Your letter to the university physics professor looks good, but there are some areas to work on. Explain your purpose for writing the letter right at the beginning. Also introduce yourself in that first paragraph. Then you should list your specific questions.

Step 6: Evaluation. AskA service experts and telementors can guide students through the evaluation process by encouraging students to assess their own use of resources and involvement in the information problem-solving process.

Example: Explanation of Evaluating Information Resource

…This Web site has a lot of great advice on studying, test taking, and writing reports. The tips on this page are geared toward students writing research papers, but they include ideas you can use for book reports too, like thinking of a main point and writing an outline, etc.

…Notice that the information from this encyclopedia is slightly different from the information in the *Encarta* article (the first encyclopedia I checked). Since the *Encarta* article has information from 1991 and this *Britannica* article has information from 1980 and 1982, I would stick with the more current *Encarta* information.

Example: Tips on Evaluating Resources and Information Problem-solving Process

…Some of the Web sites and books I have listed talk about the lima bean as a plant and some talk about it as a food. You can decide which descriptions fit best with your assignment.

When you're finished with your assignment, try to answer the following questions:
- Which types of sources answered your question best: Internet sites? Print encyclopedias?
- What other questions could you ask to get the information you're looking for?
- What did you learn about finding information on the Internet?

Since telementors are more involved with students' long-term projects and other decision-making activities, they can participate more actively in the overall evaluation process. For instance, telementoring experiences in the HP Telementoring Program often include reflection time between the student and telementor and allow for discussion of constructive criticism (Neils, 1999, phone call).

Example: Telementor Exchange Involving Evaluation of Overall Experience

Mentor: Are you happy with the way your project came out? From our discussions, it appears that you've learned a lot about creating a business plan. After some frustrations in the beginning, you found some excellent information resources to give you a jump-start on the project.

Student: It was really exciting for me to create a business plan like this, since I didn't know anything about business before. I wasn't even that interested in doing it until I started the project. Thanks for helping me write the plan and for talking with me about what you do in your business.

Sample Telecommunications Exchanges

The following examples show full messages from AskA services and telementors containing components of the Big6 process.

AskA Service Question/Answer

The following examples have been adapted from previously answered questions of exemplary AskA services. They contain resource referral and/or factual information, instructional guidance (e.g., paths to resources, tips on using information), and clear and effective language. Areas reflecting parts of the Big6 process are marked.

1. **General Reference AskA Service**
   Hello, InfoCoach:
   My name is Tammy. I'm looking for information on the 1996 Olympics. My biggest question is how do people get chosen to light the torch? Thank you very much. [1. TASK DEFINITION]

   Dear Tammy,
   Hi. Thank you for your question. In order to find information for you, I searched the World Wide Web using the Alta Vista search engine <*http://www.altavista.com*>. I typed this search term in the query box at the top of the page: [2. INFORMATION SEEKING STRATEGIES]

   +"1996 olympics" +torch [3. LOCATION AND ACCESS]

   I put "1996 Olympics" in quotes to show that it's one phrase, and I put plus signs around both phrases, because I wanted Web sites with both phrases in them. Here are some Web sites that will help answer your question:

   1. Sports Page
       http://melton.ufro.cl/news/sport.html
       This Web page has information on the history of the Olympics as well as news on the 1996 Olympics in Atlanta. In the sections "Follow the Torch" and "Olympic torch relay begins in Los Angeles," you can read about the tradition of lighting the torch. [4. USE OF INFORMATION]. It doesn't say how people are chosen to light the torch, but it does say that the name of the person chosen is kept secret by the Olympic committee.

   2. Olympics
       http://deil.lang.uiuc.edu/web.pages/holidays/Olympics.html
       This site has more information and links to other sites about Olympic history and the 1996 Olympics. You can even learn about future Olympics. Click on any of the highlighted information on the Web page to learn more [4. USE OF INFORMATION]. Note: Some of the links require that you have audio capabilities (any of the "NPR radio" sites) or a special password (*New York Times* site). Also, the "Olympics page" by Coca-Cola and the MSNBC site are not active.

3. The Olympic Movement: Home Page
   http://www.olympic.org/
   This page contains information from the International Olympic Committee (IOC). Here you can read about some of the official guidelines of the Olympics [4. USE OF INFORMATION].

These Web sites should give you a start. Take a look at them and decide which ones best answer your questions [6. EVALUATION]. Unfortunately, I wasn't able to locate much information on how people are chosen to light the torch. Perhaps after you explore these sites, you can find the answer yourself and create your own explanation [5. SYNTHESIS]. I also suggest that you ask your school library media specialist to help you find other resources on the Olympics in your school library [2. INFORMATION SEEKING STRATEGIES/3. LOCATION AND ACCESS].

Good luck and thank you for writing to InfoCoach!
Randy S., InfoCoach

2. **Subject—Math**
   Dear MathMasters,
   If a red blood cell lives about 120 days, about how many times a year is each cell replaced? [1. TASK DEFINITION]
   Susan T.

   Dear Susan,
   To answer this question, you will first need to know how many days are in a year [1. TASK DEFINITION]. If you don't know this number, you can find it by looking in an encyclopedia under the term "year" [2. INFORMATION SEEKING STRATEGIES]. Ask your library media specialist to help you find an encyclopedia in print, on CD-ROM, or the Internet that will have this answer [3. LOCATION AND ACCESS].

   To find out how many times a blood cell is replaced during a year, divide the number of days in a year by 120 days (life of a red blood cell):
   days in a year/120 days=number of times a red blood cell is replaced in one year
   [5. SYNTHESIS]
   Good luck finding an answer and thanks for asking MathMasters!
   Linda B., Math Specialist

Telementoring Episode[13]

This example is adapted from a telementoring exchange from the Electronic Emissary Project. In this example, a journalist offers suggestions to a student who is interested in learning more about news broadcasting. This exchange focuses on Big6 steps one through three (Task Definition, Information Seeking Strategies, and Location & Access). Subsequent exchanges in this scenario can focus on other Big6 steps as the student and telementor work together in all aspects of the project. For instance, the telementor can encourage the student to "use" the information by reading, taking notes, and even responding to letters from television managers; and to "synthesize" the information by writing a report on what it's like to work on a television news program, or even writing a script for a news show based on what the student learns from professionals.

13 This example is adapted from a telementor exchange between a student at Lanier Middle School in Houston, TX, and a journalist from California (*http://www.rice.edu/armadillo/Schools/Lanier/EEP/97-98/henryl.html*), arranged through the Electronic Emissary Project. Included with permission from teacher Michael Sirois. Names have been changed.

Hi,

That's neat that you're a reporter. I watch the news sometimes and I wonder if there is any way that kids like me can be on the news and help make the news more fun to watch? [1. TASK DEFINITION.]

Hello Jane,

I'm glad you're interested in being on the news and helping to make it more fun and interesting to watch. There are a couple of things I would suggest:

First, talk about this with your teacher [1. TASK DEFINITION]. I would suggest you write a letter to the General Managers of your local TV stations (all of them) [INFORMATION SEEKING STRATEGIES]. You would need to call the local library information desk to get their names and the correct spellings, or call each station and do the same [3. LOCATION & ACCESS]. You would need their addresses, as well... *OR* contact them via their Web page [3. LOCATION & ACCESS]. Every station has one and has a place for viewer comments to send via e-mail. (And remember, just because it's e-mail... your spelling and grammar are still important and should be double-checked.) I would tell the GM that you think the station should become more involved with their younger viewers; that you are, after all, the ones who will be running broadcast news in the 21st century and you think they should start participating in an effort to help you all become more critical viewers of the news, as well as participants. Tell them about the Media 2000 project [the student's class] and suggest that the station should invite two or three young people a week to come to the station and work alongside someone who works in putting the news together.

I think that's a big enough suggestion for you to consider for now. I know you can pull it off. Don't be intimidated by the TV station... they are all just regular people doing fairly regular jobs<s>. Good luck.
Best wishes,
Tanya

Communicating with Students Using the Big6™

Worksheet 3

Instructions: This worksheet is designed to assist online experts who communicate with students and educators using telecommunications activities. It is intended for use as a guide to assist online experts who are coaching students through the information problem-solving process. Keep in mind that some exchanges will concentrate on only some of the Big6 steps.

1. **Big6 Step 1—Task Definition**
   a. Focus of the question or information problem:
      - ☐ Too narrow
      - ☐ Too broad
      - ☐ On target
   b. Is a follow-up conversation required to help the student identify his or her task?
   c. In further defining the task, should the student be referred to:
      - ☐ The teacher or other adult
      - ☐ Other information resources

2. **Big6 Step 2—Information Seeking Strategies**
   Which of the following sources can help the student achieve the defined task?
   - ☐ Online expert's own knowledge
   - ☐ Other expert (e.g., AskA service, people in local community)
   - ☐ Consult school library media specialist
   - ☐ World Wide Web (see 3. Location & Access)
   - ☐ Electronic discussion group
   - ☐ Books
   - ☐ Periodicals
   - ☐ Reference sources: encyclopedia, almanac, atlas, etc.

3. **Big6 Step 3—Location & Access**
   When resources are suggested in a message, include:
   - ☐ Information path
   - ☐ Description of source
   - ☐ Citation information

4. **Big6 Step 4—Use of Information**
   Remind students to:
   - ☐ Copy and paste information from the Internet to a word processing program
   - ☐ Print and highlight
   - ☐ Read and take notes
   - ☐ Record citation information
   - ☐ Other:_____

5. **Big6 Step 5—Synthesis**

Remind student to:
- ☐ Check original assignment to make sure all requirements are met
- ☐ Check work
- ☐ Share work with others
- ☐ Write up experience (for telementoring)
- ☐ Other:_____

6. **Big6 Step 6—Evaluation**

Encourage students to answer these questions:
- ☐ What did you learn about communicating with people using the Internet?
- ☐ How well did your experience with the online expert help you complete an assignment or make certain decisions?
- ☐ How could you have written your message(s) differently so that you would receive more helpful information?
- ☐ What could you have done before you started communicating with the expert in order to get more helpful information?
- ☐ If you used information from an online expert's message in a report or other project, did you cite the message correctly?

Chapter Summary

- Telecommunications activities that place students in contact with adult experts can be very motivating for students and can help them develop important academic and developmental skills, especially in the middle grades.

- Two popular educational activities involving interpersonal exchanges are use of Ask-an-Expert (AskA) services and telementoring programs.

- AskA services are Internet-based question/answer and referral services that can assist students in answering specific questions; telementoring services match students with mentors to build long-term online relationships which may or may not involve specific instructional goals.

- Experts in telecommunications activities include:
  a) AskA service subject experts
  b) AskA service information specialists
  c) Subject area telementors
  d) Telementoring facilitators

- There are many issues for both online experts and educators to consider when participating in telecommunications activities, including purpose of activity, nature of communication, Internet safety, privacy, differences in contexts (e.g., school vs. business), preparation and management, and integration within the curriculum.

- Online experts can assist students in solving information problems by framing messages to students in a Big6 context (where appropriate) and helping students identify their place in the process.

Chapter Pathfinder

Chapter 3—Communicating with Students on the Internet

Internet Resources

Electronic Emissary Project

http://www.tapr.org/emissary/

This project maintains a database of mentors in many different areas of subject expertise and matches students and teachers to experts in a specific curriculum topic. Mentor/classroom communications are facilitated by Electronic Emissary staff members who have expertise in instruction and online projects (Harris, 1998). The project is coordinated through the University of Texas at Austin and receives support from the Texas Center for Educational Technology (TCET) and the University of Texas at Austin's College of Education (Electronic Emissary, 1998).

International Telementor Center

http://www.telementor.org

The International Telementor Center is a program at the Center for Science, Mathematics & Technology Education at the Colorado State University (CSMATE) that facilitates electronic mentoring relationships between professional adults and students worldwide. Currently, the Center manages the HP Telementor Program and the Merck Institute for Science Education.

Internet Public Library

http://www.ipl.org

A project of the University of Michigan School of Information that provides Internet users with access to resources as well as digital reference service. The IPL serves all audiences with special attention to youth needs.

Telementoring Web: Adult Experts Assisting in the Classroom

http://www.tnellen.com/cybereng/mentor/

This site links to resources about telementoring including pros and cons of telementoring, guidelines for telementoring, help for finding a telementor, and examples of telementoring programs.

ERIC Citations

Bennett, D. T. (1997). Providing role models online: Telementoring gives students real-life connections in science and beyond. *Electronic Learning, 16*(5), 50-51. (EJ 559 726). "Telementoring" programs, which are formal and informal online exchanges between students and working professionals, have flourished using e-mail. This article discusses telementoring and issues to consider (finding mentors, familiarity, frequency of exchange, preparation and facilitation, and closure) before creating a program, and the Telementoring Young Women in Science, Engineering, and Computing program for high school students.

Donlan, L. (1998). Visions of online projects dance in my head. *MultiMedia Schools*, 5(1), 20-22, 24-25. (EJ 558 544). Illustrates benefits of online class projects and describes different types of projects, including: collaborations, data collection or exchange, mentoring projects, vicarious adventures, and one-time-only events. Discusses where to find such projects and selection criteria, designing projects, and signs of success.

Gamas, W., & Nordquist, N. (1997). Expanding learning opportunities through online technology. *NASSP Bulletin*, 81(592), 16-22. (EJ 553 812). Technologies such as telecommunications, the Internet, and computer conferencing and collaboration bring students, teachers, and the community together and enhance the learning environment. Internet and computer-conferencing software (via electronic mail, Web sites, and discussion forums) allow teachers to counsel students individually, deliver information to a class, and encourage class discussion and cooperation in innovative ways. Understanding time-space configurations is essential.

Harris, J. and others. (1996). It's a simple idea, but it's not easy to do! Practical lessons in telementoring. *Learning and Leading with Technology*, 24(2), 53-57 (EJ 534 536). Describes the Electronic Emissary Project, an Internet-based interpersonal resource coordinated from the University of Texas at Austin, which matches students and teachers via e-mail with subject experts from around the world. Presents sample projects, and discusses challenges, the role of the online facilitator, and guidelines for implementing successful project-based telementoring.

Kerka, S. (1998). New perspectives on mentoring. *ERIC Digest*. 4pp. (ED 418 249). Like most institutions in a world of change, the practice of mentoring is being influenced by new forms of work, technology, and learning. Organizational trends such as downsizing, restructuring, teamwork, increased diversity, and individual responsibility for career development are contributing to a resurgent interest in mentoring in the 1990s. Many organizations are instituting formal mentoring programs as a cost-effective way to upgrade skills, enhance recruitment and retention, and increase job satisfaction. Telementoring through the Internet is emerging as a way to pair teachers and learners with subject-matter experts who can provide advice, guidance, and feedback on learning projects. Mentoring supports much of what is currently known about how individuals learn, including the socially constructed nature of learning and the importance of experiential, situational learning experiences. The most effective mentoring is that involving guided experiential learning. Because learning takes place within the social context, the interpersonal relationship of mentor and mentee is considered essential. If developing learning organizations in a learning society is a desirable social goal, mentoring can perform an important function in helping people develop their highest potential.

LaBounty, V. (1997). Reference desk on the Internet. *Book Report, 16*(2), 19. (EJ 550 885). The KidsConnect service, with 145 volunteers from 39 states and eight countries, connects librarians, teachers, and students with curriculum-related material and other information sources on the Internet. Questions received at the site (on the Web at *http://www.ala.org/ICONN/index.html* or e-mail at *askkc@ala.org*) are routed to volunteer school librarians who respond within 48 hours.

Lagace, N., & McClennen, M. (1998). Questions and quirks: Managing an Internet-based distributed reference service. *Computers in Libraries, 18*(2), 24-27. (EJ 561 382). The Internet Public Library (IPL), hosted by the University of Michigan School of Information, is an operating virtual library that answers reference questions from all over the world. Discussion includes the construct of the IPL Reference Center, how the Reference Center handles questions, and characteristics of e-mail reference service.

Lankes, R. D. (1995). AskERIC and the virtual library: Lessons for emerging digital libraries. *Internet Research, 5*(1), 56-63. (EJ 505 459). Explores major issues in creating and maintaining Internet services for AskERIC, an educational digital library started by the Educational Resources Information Center (ERIC) system. Highlights include the importance of user input to shape the service, human intermediaries, AskERIC as a virtual library, future directions, and a copy of the AskERIC brochure.

Lankes, R. D. (1998). *The virtual reference desk: Building a network of expertise for America's schools.* White Paper. 15pp. (ED 417 728). This paper presents the Virtual Reference Desk project, its current activities, and a proposed information system architecture to build a human intermediated network of expertise and experience for the K-12 community. The Virtual Reference Desk is a project headed by the ERIC Clearinghouse on Information & Technology and funded by the U.S. Department of Education's National Library of Education with support from the White House's Office of Science and Technology Policy. It seeks to study, support and improve current K-12 digital reference services, so called AskA services, as well as build a foundation for a national cooperative digital reference service. The paper demonstrates the viability of implementing a large-scale information system that directly utilizes human expertise. A preliminary technical architecture is outlined that consists of a meta-triage function to connect digital reference services, and a "shrink-wrapped" software package to help build and maintain new digital reference services.

McKee, M. B. (1995). A day in the life of a virtual librarian. *School Library Journal, 41*(4), 30-3. (EJ 501 696). The network information specialists at AskERIC, an Internet-based information service for teachers, library media specialists, administrators, and others involved in education, select and deliver information resources to the information seeker within 48 hours. A sampling of questions and responses is provided in the format of a representative day.

Morgan, N. A., & Sprague, C. (2000). An introduction to Internet resources for K-12 educators. Part II: Question answering, listservs, discussion groups, Update 2000. *ERIC Digest*. 4pp. (ED number pending). As K-12 schools connect to the Internet, a new method of communication opens up to educators and their students. This ERIC Digest describes some sample services and resources that are available to the K-12 community by electronic mail over the Internet. Question Answering services, listservs, and Usenet newsgroups are listed.

O'Neil, D. K., & Gomez, L. M. (1996). Online mentors: Experimenting in science class. *Educational Leadership*, 54(3), 39-42. (EJ 535 716). Describes a Northwestern University project exploring how to orchestrate distant mentoring ("telementoring") relationships between science students and workplace scientists. The goal was to develop an audience of (volunteer) scientists to offer students ongoing advice and criticism. Challenges included finding appropriate volunteers, sustaining activities, designing assessments and incentives, and maintaining communication.

Pack, T. (1996). A guided tour of the Internet Public Library: Cyberspace's unofficial library offers outstanding collections of Internet resources. *Database*, 19(5), 52-56. (EJ 532 868). Describes the Internet Public Library, developed at the University of Michigan's School of Information and Library Studies. Site highlights include the reference center; the reading room, which includes materials in full-text; youth and teen services; professional information for librarians; links to Web search engines; a Multiuser Object Oriented (MOO) reference area; and a virtual exhibit hall.

Ryan, S. (1996). Reference service for the Internet community: A case study of the Internet Public Library Reference Division. *Library & Information Science Research*, 18(3), 241-59. (EJ 532 939). Examines the creation of the Internet Public Library Reference Division in the historical context of librarians' efforts to integrate the use of technologies with reference services. Discussion considers ways that librarians have successfully incorporated new technologies and makes recommendations for use of the Reference Division and Internet usage for the reference process in general.

Sanchez, B., & Harris, J. (1996). Online mentoring—a success story. *Learning and Leading with Technology*, 23(8), 57-60. (EJ 526 329). Describes the Internet-based Electronic Emissary Project that helps teachers locate other Internet account holders who are subject matter experts in different disciplines for the purpose of setting up curriculum-based electronic exchanges among experts and elementary and secondary students and teachers.

Serving the Internet public: The Internet Public Library. (1996). *Electronic Library, 14*(2), 122-26. (EJ 526 267). Describes the Internet Public Library (IPL), which was developed at the School of Information and Library Studies at the University of Michigan to be a library for Internet users. Highlights include mission statement and goals, funding, staffing with volunteers, future possibilities, IPL services, and statement of principles.

Tobiason, K. (1997). Taking by giving: KidsConnect and your media center. *Technology Connection, 4*(6), 10-11. (EJ 554 221). Discusses KidsConnect (KC), an initiative of the American Association of School Librarians (AASL) volunteer service to help children access and use the information available on the Internet effectively and efficiently. Describes the benefits to volunteers: improved Internet skills; knowledge of Internet-related resources; familiarity with worthwhile educational Web sites; collegial support; the thrill of information seeking and retrieval; and professional renewal.

Designing and Providing Content on the Internet for K–12 Students

Designing and Providing Content on the Internet for K–12 Students

Chapter Profile

This chapter provides suggestions for developing content on the Internet that can help K-12 students develop their information problem-solving skills. This can include school-based Web sites highlighting students' original work or study guides, Web pages from organizations specializing in a certain subject area, archives of students' questions and experts' responses, and online courses and tutorials. The chapter describes some different types of Internet resources designed for K-12 students and offers guidelines and examples for designing content that enhances learning and promotes an information problem-solving approach.

Develop and provide content on the Internet for K-12 students that enhances learning and promotes information problem-solving.

Before reading this chapter, you should be able to:
1. Design and develop content for the Web.
2. Perform or oversee production of a Web-based resource.

This chapter will prepare you to:
1. Understand the importance of incorporating instructional design features and promoting information problem-solving in the design of Internet-based content for K-12 students.
2. Identify different types of Internet resources designed for K-12 students.
3. State types of people who design content on the Internet for K-12 students.
4. Identify instructional design and information problem-solving considerations involved in the design of content on the Internet for K-12 students.
5. Design content for the Internet according to instructional design guidelines and incorporate components of the Big6 information problem-solving model.
6. Identify Big6 features in existing Web sites.

Designing Content on the Internet for K-12 Students

The World Wide Web offers motivating and effective learning experiences to students through its multimedia features and its ability to link to information from various locations on the Internet. Designers of student-oriented Web services—a group that ranges from classroom teachers to commercial information providers—have the exciting opportunity to present conceptual information in creative ways and to be leaders in helping children develop information problem-solving skills.

Educational content providers have started to lean toward the World Wide Web because of increased editorial control and revenues (Weiss, 1996). What does this mean for students? Certainly, this means the availability of more information, but it also means more material for students to wade through on the way to answering questions and completing projects. For Web page designers, this means more responsibility to incorporate good instructional design features and to promote information literacy skills and lifelong learning (Lindsay, 1996). This chapter focuses on ways that educational Web page designers can provide the most effective instructional products to kids—by offering high-quality, well-organized educational content and by guiding users through an information problem-solving model.

Web Resources for K-12 Students

There are literally thousands of educational resources on the Internet of widely varying quality and purpose. Web sites labeled "educational" include anything from interactive games promoting color-identification and pattern-building to online magazines highlighting student work to lists of Web links categorized by school subjects.

Many educational Web sites can be broken down into these categories:

■ Games, crafts, activities
■ Online magazines or other Web-based publications written for children
■ Facts, explanations, and descriptions
■ Interactive services such as expert question-answering and telementoring
■ Online courses and tutorials
■ Pointers to Internet and non-Internet resources

The quality of educational Internet resources depends on many factors: accuracy, quality and organization of content; navigational features (ease of moving around the site); use of visual effects; authority of content providers.

This chapter makes a distinction between educational and instructional resources (Internet as well as non-Internet). Educational resources are developed to assist students in gaining knowledge in a certain subject or skill area, while instructional resources are developed to help students achieve a defined goal. Educational resources are obviously more general and they appeal to a wider audience, while instructional resources are more focused and include strategies for gauging student performance (or helping students measure their own performance). Developers of both types of Internet resources can benefit from the suggestions in the following sections.

Information Mentor Spotlight: Internet Content Developers

With the availability of Web editing software such as Netscape _Composer_, Microsoft _Front Page_, and even some word processing programs such as Microsoft _Word_, it is possible for even the least-techie of us to create useful, attractive content on the Web for K-12 students. People developing Web sites for K-12 students today include:

- Practicing K-12 educators
- Students
- Software developers and programmers
- Information professionals
- Representatives of commercial and non-profit organizations, educational institutions, government agencies, and other entities that maintain a collection of resources or information services
- Independent researchers
- Anyone with Internet access

Issues in Web Development for K-12 Audiences

As previously noted, there are many factors aside from the nature of the content that make an educational or instructional Web site a quality resource. This section discusses some of these factors in terms of instructional design and information problem-solving considerations.

Instructional Design Considerations

Web sites can be evaluated in terms of their potential to help students learn. Those Web sites considered instructional should contain certain features to help students reach specific instructional goals. According to El-Tigi and Branch (1997), Web sites designed by educators for use in the classroom should provide[14] (p. 23):

- Interactivity between student and instructor
- Student control of information he or she processes
- Feedback from the instructor (to measure knowledge).

Small and Arnone (1999a) focus their Web evaluation criteria on the motivational quality of a resource. According to the authors, a Web site should include features that "make using it an enjoyable experience" and encourage students to explore, revisit the site, and recommend it to others (p. 25). Small and Arnone have developed three WebMAC (Web site Motivational Analysis Checklist) Evaluation Instruments for K-12 students in order to help them identify the motivational quality of Web sites. The WebMAC instruments, designed for elementary, middle, and high school students, allow students to score different Web site features and tally scores for a final comprehensive motivational rating of the site. These checklists can also be used by Web site designers to help them incorporate motivational features, such as (Small & Arnone, 1998):

- Attractive colors, background, graphics, and layout
- Accurate, relevant, clear, and current information

---

14 See El-Tigi and Branch, 1997, for suggestions in designing Web sites to maximize these instructional features.

- Consistent style, language, and navigational features (e.g., buttons)
- Examples of concepts presented
- Appropriate use of humor
- Accessible "help" function
- Functional links to other sites
- Logical and well-communicated organization of site
- Use of credible information sources
- Clear purpose
- Variety of type of information
- Simple and clear directions
- Reasonable download time for graphics and other files.

There are many other useful Web site evaluation guides (such as Schrock, 1996) that may be considered by those designing educational or instructional Web resources. See Appendix C for a list of Web site evaluation resources.

Incorporating Big6™ Skills

Cottrell and Eisenberg (1997) recommend using the Big6 to design Web pages to facilitate users' information seeking and problem-solving processes. Relying on the Big6 not only benefits Web page users (such as K-12 students), but it also guides designers by helping them define the user audience and anticipate users' information problem-solving needs at different stages of the process. For instance, students engaged in Task Definition will examine a site for its potential usefulness as they seek to identify an information problem and potentially useful resources. To guide students at this stage, Web site designers should clearly state the site's purpose and help students define information needs through thought-provoking questions and pointers to specific resources on the site (see Table 4-1 for suggestions to help students at each Big6 step through Web site design).

The following section provides guidelines for using the Big6 and instructional design considerations in developing Web resources for K-12 students.

Guidelines for Designing Web Resources for Students

There are many resources available that offer tips on the technical aspects of designing Web sites. Other resources offer criteria for users to evaluate sites (See Appendix E: Locating And Designing School Web Pages, and Appendix C: Evaluation of Internet Sites). This section guides Web page designers through the decisions that occur during the planning stages, before developing hypertext or graphics. These planning guidelines are based upon models of instructional design and information problem-solving and are focused on designing the most appropriate product for a particular audience. The following planning model is the same one that is used in Chapter 1. Educators and others may incorporate suggestions from both chapters when designing Web pages for classroom instruction and independent learning. (Also see El-Tigi and Branch [1997, p. 27-28] for a Web-Based Learning Design Model that presents additional guidelines for creating instructional Web resources.) As you complete the following process, record all your decisions to make the process go more smoothly now and in future projects.

Designers who are preparing educational and instructional Web sites should answer the following questions:

1. Who is the intended audience?
2. What is the site's purpose?
3. How should the site be organized?
4. How will the plan become a product?
5. How will it work?
6. Am I all done?

1. Who is the Intended Audience?

Before any content is developed, it is crucial to identify the intended primary audience for the Web site. Unless restrictions are established (i.e., passwords), anyone in the world can potentially access the page, but to present the information most effectively, it should be targeted to a specific group: all sixth-graders in the United States studying the Constitution, students at Acorn Elementary, K-12 students and parents around the world with questions about science.

After an intended audience is identified, a designer should conduct background analysis and research on the population, or a sample population, to examine the following issues:

- **National or local academic standards:** (See Appendix D: Academic Standards on the Internet.) Standards will help shape content and will help ensure that Web page designers, educators, students, and parents are working toward a common goal. Some work is already being done to map existing educational Web resources (e.g., lesson plans) with local, state, and national content standards (Sutton, 1999). Users are looking for Web resources that can support academic standards.

- **Skill levels and capabilities of target age group:** What is the general reading level? This will help determine the language used to present information and the concepts communicated. Will any students in the audience require special accommodations for visual or auditory disabilities or lower reading/literacy skills? Chances are "yes," unless you're dealing with an extremely small, isolated population. See "National Center for Accessible Media," *http://www.wgbh.org/ncam*, for ideas on planning Web sites for people with disabilities or low literacy skills or minority language users (Lindsay, 1996).[15]

- **Attitudes/opinions toward content area:** Since the Web has the potential to increase students' motivation to learn, why not interview some members of the intended audience to determine how they feel about the given content area or currently available resources? For instance, do students find chemistry boring as it is taught in their text book? Are they interested in learning more about art history? Starting from the same perspective as your audience can help you communicate your message more effectively.

- **Technical capabilities:** To accommodate all browser types, it is safest to plan for the lowest common denominator—especially if gearing toward classroom use. Offer a choice between graphics and text, or restrict fancy graphics if they overshadow the content (Lindsay, 1996).

In addition to examining the audience, it is helpful to survey other Internet sites covering your content area to determine what is currently available and what appears to be missing.

---

15 Also see CAST, Inc.'s "Bobby" site (*http://www.cast.org/bobby/*).

2. *What is the Site's Purpose?*

The purpose of an educational Web page, or any instructional product, can be defined in terms of what the learner should be able to achieve as a result of interacting with it. This can be done by creating three types of statements: needs, goals and objectives. The "need" is some problem that can be solved possibly through successful Web page design. The conclusions found in your initial research will help you to identify a need.

Example: Need

"National standards for high school students include understanding the importance of participating in a democratic society. However, many high school students do not understand these concepts, and there are few resources that motivate students of this age group to do so."

From this statement, you can create goals and objectives to guide your content. Your goal should reflect an academic standard or curriculum goal and should imply some type of observable action or behavior.

Example: Goal

"High school students in the United States will write articles for and edit an Internet-based newsletter discussing current issues in public affairs and constitutional democracy."

To achieve this goal, students will need to perform a variety of other skills that may be organized as components of the Big6 process. These skills are planned out in the form of objectives, each matching a Big6 step where appropriate. Objectives not only set out what the student, or Web page user, should do, but will help guide the Web page designer to present and organize content.

Example: Objectives

Students will:
1. Identify a question related to current events dealing with public affairs or constitutional democracy (Task Definition).
2. Record possible print, electronic, Internet, and human sources that can answer the question in a journal or database (Information Seeking Strategies).
3. Participate in an e-mail discussion with a mentoring politician to discuss how specific problems are addressed (Location & Access).
4. Write notes based on resources consulted and e-mail discussions (Use of Information).
5. Write an article on the issue discussing common viewpoints and personal opinions (Synthesis).
6. E-mail peers to discuss successes and areas for improvement regarding the project (Evaluation).

During this stage, Web designers should consult with classroom teachers and library media specialists to ensure that the proposed resources match goals and content areas covered in local curricula.

3. How Should the Site be Organized?

At this point, the purpose has been defined as a goal with several objectives; the blueprint for designing an instructional or educational resource has begun. Now, the designer must make decisions regarding how to present the content so student users can achieve the objectives. This table, adapted from Cottrell and Eisenberg (1997, p. 54, 56), offers some suggestions for supporting each Big6 step through Web site design. Specific methods will differ depending on age group, content, and other factors. As demonstrated in the following table, items in step 2, Information Seeking Strategies, and step 3, Location & Access, may sometimes overlap, since both steps concentrate on helping students identify and access sources within and beyond the Web site.

Table 4-1: Big6™ Steps and Web Site Components

Big6™ Step	Web Site provides...
1. Task Definition	■ Questions (FAQ) or controversial statements to stimulate curiosity (headlines from newspapers, statistics) ■ Explanation of structure, purpose, and intended audience of the site to show what kinds of questions are addressed and what types of resources are available ■ Directions according to user needs ("if you need x, then see y")
2. Information Seeking Strategies	■ Lists of topics covered at site (e.g., site map or guide) ■ Guidelines on general information sources that are appropriate for different types of questions (show sample questions and sample resources) ■ Pointers to a select list of related resources (e.g., Web links, bibliographies); annotate if possible ■ Contextual information for all information included (e.g., label/title, date, source) ■ Suggestions of keywords, synonyms for searching
3. Location & Access	■ Pointers to helpful starting points on page or site (e.g., internal links, search tools, intermediary pages with content descriptions) ■ Accessibility to the site (register site in Web search engines and indexes so users can easily locate it) ■ Options for access within the site (e.g., views by audience, topic, etc.) ■ Information on how to access external information sources if not directly available (e.g., refer student to school library media specialist)
4. Use of Information	■ Headings and sections to separate and organize information ■ Clear presentation of information on site (question/answer format, headings) ■ Graphics and backgrounds that don't distract from the content ■ Appropriate format, media for particular purpose ■ Minimum download time, common file formats, and command sets for graphics and other files ■ Explanation of requirements or restrictions on use of site ■ Different versions for different audiences (e.g., no-frames and no-graphics options) ■ Examples of how to use information provided to achieve certain goals ■ Citation guidelines for information on and off site ■ Tips for taking notes

Big6™ Step	Web Site provides...
5. Synthesis	■ Style guidelines and ideas for writing articles, papers, presentations ■ Tips for solving problems (math formulas, science experiments, etc.) ■ Examples of good synthesis in content, presentation and organization
6. Evaluation	■ Series of questions regarding resources used, final product and whole information problem-solving process ■ Periodic survey of users ■ Mechanisms for users to share feedback (e.g., feedback form, guest book, e-mail address) ■ Options for additional resources and actions if original information problem wasn't solved ■ Collection of statistics and log files to quantify use of site and to determine types of users.

Other considerations include:

■ Interaction—Will there be direct communication between the user and a Web site representative such as an AskA service (see Chapter 3)? Will there be feedback on student progress toward objectives?

■ Curriculum-integration—Will the Web page be used in conjunction with classroom lessons led by teachers? If so, consider creating sample lesson plans to help teachers integrate your Web resource into the curriculum (see Chapter 1).

■ Basic elements—At this stage, you can create a draft of the elements to appear on each page, including placement of logo, graphics, links, and content.

4. *How Will the Plan Become a Product?*

This is where the technical expertise comes in: writing HTML code, inserting graphics, creating links. Keep in mind that in addition to providing subject content and guidance in information problem-solving, your site itself is an information resource. In developing your site, you are creating a model by which students should judge other Web sites and resources. Below is a list of items to consider during Website development, as compiled from several collections of Web site evaluation criteria (see Appendix C: Evaluation of Internet Sites for more evaluation criteria):

a) **Stay simple:** It is better to include a small amount of clearly organized text on each page than to bombard the reader with too much text or graphics at once. Choose graphics that are appropriate for the tone and subject of the page, and place them in areas that do not interfere with the main text. Also, make sure the images don't take too long to load.

b) **Describe information:** Titles and headings should accurately describe the contents presented. When listing linked sites or additional information, it is important to use specific terms. This list should describe not only the general subject-area of the linked information, but the scope and the format as well. (In other words, will "Frog Stuff" lead to an explanation of frog anatomy or links to frog jokes?)

c) **Present information at the level of comprehension:** Avoid using unnecessary jargon, abbreviations, or acronyms. Refer users to Internet-based or print glossaries and dictionaries when using terms beyond the expected comprehension level.

d) **Provide easy navigation:** Allow links back to the main page from all pages on the site and link to other pages on the site in a logical manner.

e) **Be accurate and give credit:** Make sure all information is accurate and that all terms are spelled correctly. Also, include proper citations when borrowing information from other sources.

f) **Be objective:** Avoid personal or organizational biases when possible. When explaining a controversial opinion, clarify its source and where it fits in with the issue as a whole.

g) **Show authority:** Include author's name and expertise associated with the content on the page. Mention awards or reviews from online reviewing agencies (Schrock, 1996).

h) **Encourage feedback:** Allow users to contact the author to ask questions or make comments and suggestions.

i) **List date last updated and other citation information:** Include name of Web page author(s) (individuals or organizations), date created and updated (the more current, the better), and information regarding source of content.

5. *Will It Work?*

The only way to really judge the effectiveness of a Web site is to test it. Before allowing full access to the site, make it available to a portion of your intended audience (for instance, assign passwords or limit publicity) and run a pilot test. Let the users explore the site freely and make comments, or have them participate in a guided activity. Have the audience judge the site according to a list of criteria, such as the one mentioned previously. Make sure the site is tested on various browsers to ensure readability and usability by all. Revise the site based on test results.

Examples of Web site evaluation instruments that can be used during a pilot testing stage include WebMAC (Small & Arnone, 1999b) and Kathleen Schrock's Critical Evaluation Surveys (Schrock, 1998).

6. *Am I All Done?*

Not exactly. Once a Web site is available to the public, quality must be continually maintained. Create a system for revising and updating contents and features based on user response and other changes and developments. Closely monitor academic standards and trends, and survey your user population to make sure you continue to meet user needs.

Another form of ongoing Web site evaluation and maintenance involves measuring the number of visitors to the site. This information is sometimes requested by funding sources of Web sites as a way to assess the need for their contributions (or the audience for their advertisements). Many Web site owners collect statistics on how many times the site is "hit," or the documents and images on a site are downloaded to the user's client software. This method can be unreliable because it does not account for multiple file transfers during the loading of one Web page during a single user's visit. However, some of the information is helpful for ongoing site maintenance, such as identifying Web site locations that are most often visited (Lankes & Kasowitz, 1998).

Examples: Big6™ and Web Page Design

The Big6 is promoted in existing educational Web sites, sometimes without the authors even realizing it. Some sites present Big6 steps more clearly than others. This section highlights two examples of Web sites that incorporate the Big6 steps successfully. The Ask Dr. Math site from the Math Forum is geared primarily toward K-12 students and happens to incorporate Big6 concepts in its organization, content and communication features. The Big6 Project Pages from St. Agnes Academy in Houston, TX, were designed specifically to guide students at this college prep school "through a process of critical thinking, skill building, and problem-solving" in completing school projects (Buehler & Jones, 1998, p.1).

Ask Dr. Math, Math Forum

http://www.mathforum.com/dr.math/

Ask Dr. Math is an AskA service for K-12 students focusing on all areas of math from addition to algorithms. Student questions are answered by more than 225 volunteer mathematicians and math students from around the world. The Ask Dr. Math Web site provides access to responses from previously asked questions including sets of Frequently Asked Questions. Ask Dr. Math is a project of the Math Forum, "an online math education community center" (The Math Forum, 1999).

Big6 Step 1—Task Definition

Upon entering the Ask Dr. Math home page, the user is immediately presented with a question: "Have a K-12 Math Question?" Not only does this clearly (and concisely) define the purpose of the Web site, but it prompts the user to think of how to phrase the information problem. In addition, the page organizes its information into different grade levels—elementary school, middle school, high school, college and beyond—which helps the user refine the question according to general math curriculum areas and skill levels.

Big6 Step 2—Information Seeking Strategies

Just beneath the opening question, users are given a choice of where to go to find answers to their questions: "Search archives," "Dr. Math FAQ," or "Send to Dr. Math." Users can browse information in the archives within specific grade levels (as presented above). Archives are organized by topic within each grade level (e.g., square roots, logarithms, etc.) and then by a heading representing a specific question and answer set (e.g., "An Explanation of Pascal's Triangle," "Cutting An Equal Number of Slices of Cake").

The site also provides pointers to other resources for additional help. These lists of links can be found in a few different locations:

- Ask Dr. Math question submission page—a list of resources to try before sending a question (*http://mathforum.com/dr.math/ask.html*).
- Quick Reference Sheet (*http://mathforum.com/special.html*)—a matrix that organizes resources by topic, audience, features, and other categories.
- Math Forum Math Resources by Subject (*http://mathforum/math.topics.html*)—a list of external Web sites.

Big6 Step 3—Location & Access

Besides providing direct links to the information, the site provides suggestions as to where a user should begin to look. On pages listing messages on a particular topic, there is a red star accompanied by the explanation, "Interesting answers or good places to begin browsing." With this tip, a student just starting on a search can scroll right down to a question with a red star.

In addition to the friendly and varied browsing environment, the site offers a search engine (*http://mathforum.com/mathgrepform.html*) to help students locate information on specific topics. This way, a student can search for information in a particular area without having to know the category or grade level in which Web site designers have catalogued it.

Big6 Step 4—Use of Information

This site maximizes the student's ability to interact with the information provided through minimal use of graphics and simple white backgrounds, logical categories of topics for easy navigation, clear explanations of concepts and examples, and titles of pages for easy identification and citation.

The page that allows students to send their own questions to Dr. Math (*http://mathforum.com/dr.math/ask.html*) contains helpful information including directions for asking appropriate questions (i.e., those relating to math topics covered in grades K-12), guidelines on using Ask Dr. Math in the classroom, links to other resources including Ask Dr. Math archives and FAQs, and instructions for completing the question submission form. This page clearly states that only a portion of submitted questions are answered; this sets users' expectations and encourages the student to consult available resources for an answer before submitting a question to the math experts.

Big6 Step 5—Synthesis

Responses to student questions on the Web site contain suggestions for presenting and organizing the information. For example, an answer to an addition question from an elementary student includes a tip on writing an addition problem so that the ones, tens, and hundreds digits line up. In the answer, each column of digits was added separately until the answer was presented. In order to make sure this student and other readers understood the concept, the author of the message included more similar problems for practice (*http://mathforum.com/dr.math/problems/3.digit.adding.html*).

Big6 Step 6—Evaluation

Some of the messages encourage students to contact the site again if they have more questions or have trouble understanding the concepts in the message. The visitor to the site is encouraged to send in a question, if he or she was unable to find an answer in the archives— "Still have a question?" This illustrates that the information problem-solving process can continue after an unsuccessful search and that information is not always found in the first source consulted. It also encourages students to rephrase or refine information problems and questions.

The Ask Dr. Math Web site also provides a periodic user survey to collect information on user demographics and interests relating to the site.

Big6™ Project Pages, St. Agnes Academy

http://www.st-agnes.org/library/projects/bigsix.html

St. Agnes Academy is a private college prep school in Houston, Texas. Library media specialists and teachers collaborate to develop Web pages that guide students through the Big6 process in the context of a given assignment (Buehler & Jones, 1998). This is an example of an Internet resource created by school faculty to meet specific curriculum goals. In addition to providing a useful research framework for students, the development of the Big6 Project Pages has helped teachers at St. Agnes Academy construct richer and more effective assignments and library media specialists to work more closely with subject area teachers (Buehler & Jones, 1998).

Each Big6 Project Page includes the list of Big6 steps and links to information and resources that can help students achieve each step in the context of a subject area assignment. The pages are incorporated into instruction by classroom teachers and library media specialists.

This example is based upon one Big6 Project Page for an 11th grade English assignment on F. Scott Fitzgerald and the 1920s to accompany the students' reading of *The Great Gatsby*. See: *http://www.st-agnes.org/library/projects/gatsby.html*

Big6 Step 1—Task Definition

A link from the main page—"What am I supposed to do?"—leads to a detailed explanation of assignment requirements. The requirements include goals, project due date, list of possible research topics (e.g., prohibition/gangsters, fashion/music/dance/movies, women's suffrage, etc.), and criteria for grading the assignment.

The question "What information do I need?" reminds students to think about the type of information that will be required to complete the assignment (e.g., historical facts).

Big6 Step 2—Information Seeking Strategies

The link—"What are the possible sources of information I can use?"—leads to lists of resources available in the school library (books, magazines, CD-ROMs) as well as links to suggested Web sites with information on the general topic area. Instructions for accessing library resources are also included such as reminders to use the online library catalog and to consult reserve and reference books.

The question "What are the best sources for this assignment?" prompts students to prioritize from the list of possible sources.

Big6 Step 3—Location & Access

This section of the Big6 Project Page offers guidance in two areas: where to find suggested or selected sources and how to use the sources. Links are provided to online catalogs at the Saint Agnes Academy Library, Houston Public Library and other public libraries, as well as tips on using Internet search engines.

Big6 Step 4—Use of Information

The question "How will I record information?" prompts students to think about taking notes and highlighting important information that pertains to their topic. A link from the question "How will I evaluate the information?" leads to a Web page from the UCLA College Library with some points to consider when evaluating Web resources.

Big6 Step 5—Synthesis

The question "How is the information best presented?" allows students to revisit their original assignment for any special presentation requirements (e.g., multi-media presentation, one-page typed summary) and to organize their information and thoughts into a final product. "How will I credit my sources?" links to a guide to citing electronic sources from Wolfgram Memorial Library at Widener University.

Big6 Step 6—Evaluation

The questions "How well did my product turn out?" and "Was I happy with my process of finding and using information?" allow students to reflect on their experiences with the overall assignment. A Web-based evaluation form is included in the Big6 Project Page to collect students' thoughts on the effectiveness and efficiency of the Big6 process for this particular assignment and specific types of resources.

Other

Big6 Project Pages can be easily integrated into classroom instruction allowing many opportunities to teach information skills in context, such as (Buehler & Jones, 1998):
- The overall Big6 process
- Use of specific information resources and tools (including Internet search engines and browsers)
- Evaluation of Internet and other resources
- Use of presentation tools such as color printers, scanners, and *PowerPoint*.

Designing and Providing Internet Content for K-12 Students Using the Big6™

Worksheet 4

Instructions: This worksheet is intended to help information mentors design content on the Internet for K-12 students.

1. **Who is the audience?**

   Intended audience characteristics: _____

   _____

   _____

   _____

   Consider:
   - ☐ National and local academic standards
   - ☐ Skill levels and capabilities of target age group
   - ☐ Attitudes and opinions toward content area
   - ☐ Technical capabilities
   - ☐ Survey other related Internet sites
   - ☐ Consult with classroom teachers and library media specialists to ensure the proposed resource matches academic goals and standards.

2. **What is the purpose?**

   Describe the main goal of the resource: _____

   _____

   _____

   _____

   Objectives

   Describe what the students will be expected to accomplish and the corresponding Big6 step.

Objective	Big6™ Step(s)

3. **How will it be organized?**

Big Six Step	Web Site provides...
1. Task Definition	
2. Information Seeking Strategies	
3. Location & Access	
4. Use of Information	
5. Synthesis	
6. Evaluation	

4. **How Will the Plan Become a Product?**
   - ☐ Stay simple
   - ☐ Describe information
   - ☐ Present information at level of comprehension
   - ☐ Provide easy navigation
   - ☐ Be accurate and give credit
   - ☐ Be objective
   - ☐ Show authority by documenting
   - ☐ Encourage feedback
   - ☐ List date last updated and other citation information

5. **Will It Work?**
   Pilot test options:
   - ☐ Limit access to test group
   - ☐ Structured survey
   - ☐ Unstructured evaluation
   - ☐ Testers judge according to criteria
   - ☐ Test on multiple browsers
   - ☐ Revise based on test results

6. **Am I All Done?**
   - ☐ Create plan for ongoing revisions and updates
   - ☐ Monitor academic standards and trends
   - ☐ Schedule regular surveys of user population
   - ☐ Measure Web use statistics

Chapter Summary

- Designers of Web sites for K-12 students should incorporate instructional design features and promote information problem-solving skills.
- Educational resources (Internet or non-Internet) are designed to assist students in gaining knowledge in a subject or skill, while instructional resources are designed to help students achieve a defined goal.
- Those who develop instructional or educational Internet resources for K-12 students can include educators, students, information professionals, commercial information providers, researchers, and anyone with Internet access.
- Web site features that reflect good instructional design include those that support interactivity between the student and instructor, student control of learning, and feedback from the instructor, as well as motivate students to learn.
- Big6 Skills can guide Internet content providers by helping them define the user audience and anticipate users' information problem-solving needs at different stages of the process.
- In designing content for the Web, consider the user audience, identify the purpose, organize the content and features to enhance learning, develop the final product from a plan, test the resource on a defined audience, and plan for ongoing evaluation and maintenance of the site.
- Existing sites can be assessed according to use of Big6 steps and general information problem-solving components.

Chapter Pathfinder

Chapter 4—Designing and Providing Internet Content for K-12 Students

Internet Resources

Delivering Instruction on the World Wide Web
http://www.svsu.edu/~mcmanus/papers/wbi.html
This paper, written by Thomas Fox McManus of University of Texas at Austin, is directed toward educators but is useful for anyone interested in designing and delivering Web-based instruction. Topics include getting started with the Web, creating instruction, and creating Web pages. Instructional systems design models are used as a basis for discussion.

School Web Page Development Guide
http://www.massnetworks.org/~nicoley/schools/
This page contains some general guidelines for creating school home pages as well as a list of content ideas to help you select appropriate material for your own school's home page. It's best to pick and choose from the list to select the items that make the most sense for the type of school, the number of people available to create and maintain the home page, and the interests of the Web page creators (excerpt from site).

Tips for Developing School Web Pages
http://www.siec.k12.in.us/~west/online/index.html
Find tips for developing your own content-rich, visually attractive Web page. Topics include copyright issues, tips to help you determine what kind of Web page you want to design, six easy steps to follow, how to evaluate your Web page, and how to announce your project to the world.

ERIC Citations

Buchanan, M. (1997). So you want to write a school home page but don't know where to begin. *Technology Connection, 4*(4), 26-27. (EJ 550 879). Discusses aspects of school home pages: school policy, parental involvement and concerns, Internet access and commercial providers, HTML programming, links to other Web pages, graphics, and the importance of proofreading.

Clark, B. I. and others. (1997). *Creating Web pages: Is anyone considering visual literacy?* In: VisionQuest: Journeys toward Visual Literacy. Selected Readings from the Annual Conference of the International Visual Literacy Association (28th, Cheyenne, Wyoming, October, 1996); see IR 018 353. 9pp. (ED 408 990). The purpose of this study was: (1) to look at the design, aesthetics, and functionality of educational and noneducational Web pages from the perspective of visual literacy; and (2) to evaluate printed and online materials that are used as resources by professionals and nonprofessionals to create these Web pages. These "how to" manuals were evaluated for their discussion of good screen design, the use of graphics and icons as communication, backgrounds, hypertext, linking, and overall understanding of publishing on the World Wide Web. The Web pages were divided into major categories and subcategories. The educational categories included K-12 schools and colleges/universities, and the noneducation categories included commercial, publications and communications, informational and cultural, and personal Web pages. Two evaluation instruments were developed: one contained 21 questions for evaluating online and printed resource materials; a second evaluation instrument contained 57 questions that were embedded in the categories of design, graphics, text, and color. These categories were divided into aesthetics and functionality. Initial data analysis indicates a wide range of quality in all the sites. The commercial sites developed by professionals contained animations and sophisticated graphics that met the evaluation criteria, but tended to target a narrow group of people; some of the Web pages were well designed and met the needs of the general user. Evaluation of the printed and online materials indicates a strong agreement in the use of how to create in HTML language and the technical aspects of using specific image formats for World Wide Web publishing.

Haile, P. J. (1998). *Teacher-student collaboration to create a curriculum-based Web page.* 41pp. Paper presented at the Annual Meeting of the American Association of Colleges for Teacher Education (50th, New Orleans, LA, February 25-28, 1998). (ED 418 071). This paper describes a Hofstra University (New York) project, funded by the Corporation for Public Broadcasting (CPB), that involved teacher-student collaboration to develop a curriculum-based Web page. Seventeen school districts participated in a 12-hour training program to teach school-based teams (one school library media specialist and two students) to create World Wide Web home pages for their schools. The home pages were designed to be curriculum-based sites for augmenting classroom instruction. Teams attended Hofstra University for four biweekly, hands-on sessions on creating and maintaining home pages. Each team prepared two projects. At the conclusion, three outside experts critiqued teams' efforts and provided constructive feedback. Participants completed short questionnaires on their reactions to the project. School administrators completed telephone surveys on their reactions. School teams' Web pages were reviewed during the following academic year. Several media specialists and students were greatly empowered by the training. Most teams incorporated two or more interesting features into their Web pages. A quarter of the teams had difficulty with very rudimentary aspects of the task, and the short training did not provide enough time, with guidance and instruction, to succeed. The project did not result in any changes in the area of curriculum. The two appendices present a sample letter to the Superintendent of Schools explaining the Web Page Training Program and the CPB grant curriculum.

Hall, A., & Basile, B. (1997). *Building student-centered Web sites in the K-12 Classroom.* 55pp. (ED 416 831). This paper examines the process of constructing a student-centered World Wide Web site and provides recommendations for improving this process. In the project, preservice teachers instructed the fifth grade students about how to design and develop a Web site on weather. The topics of the sessions included Internet ethics, using the Web, pre-planning and storyboards, and Web site construction. The project modeled the use of the Web in conjunction with classroom instruction. The goals of this project were to build a student-centered Web site; to use technology to reinforce instruction; and to provide students and teachers with a curriculum-based Web site that is a useful and relevant resource. The paper includes six chapters: (1) "Introduction"; (2) "Background" including unproductive roles of technology in the past, barriers to use of technology; educational applications of the Internet, the World Wide Web, advantages to building student-centered Web sites, cooperative learning, collaboration methods for Internet projects, evaluation methods, Web page design, and HTML (HyperText Markup Language); (3) "Purpose and Rationale" of use of technology in instruction; (4) "Method" of the project, which consisted of tutoring a small group of eight students about the process so that they in turn could eventually teach their classmates; (5) "Evaluation Methodology"; and (6) "Summary and Conclusions." Appendices include: a list of components in a complete storyboard, Weather Wizards Website, Interview questions for participating students and Interview questions for Inservice teachers.

Lindsay, L. (1996). *Web page design*. Peru, NE: Peru State College Library. 9pp (ED 399 971). Designing a Web home page involves many decisions that affect how the page will look, the kind of technology required to use the page, the links the page will provide, and kinds of patrons who can use the page. The theme of information literacy needs to be built into every Web page; users need to be taught the skills of sorting and applying information to their individual needs. Web page design should involve: (1) planning ahead and writing a style sheet to define the who, what, and how of the pages; (2) keeping the pages simple; (3) designing the pages for fast use and allowing the user to have a choice between text and graphics; (4) making the pages readable; (5) showing the interdisciplinary and hierarchical nature of information and knowledge; and (6) keeping the links up-to-date. While HTML programming does not define the document structure as desktop publishing, the time is quickly coming when the principles of desktop publishing will be used in Web publishing. The Web designer who wants to design a Web page that all browsers can use will use the HTML2 standard. There are resources designed to help with a home page and to evaluate information on the Internet for use when designing Web pages. Two such resources are highlighted, as well as a sample of the Peru State College Library (Nebraska) home page.

Monahan, B., & Tomko, S. (1996). How schools can create their own Web pages. *Educational Leadership, 54*(3), 37-38. (EJ 535 715). Schools in two New York State counties are creating Web home pages with little money or technical expertise. Approaches to Web page construction include using commercially developed software (like *Pagemaker* or *Claris Works*); trying out downloaded shareware programs; using an online service (America Online, Prodigy, or Compuserve); and programming in HTML (hypertext markup language).

Murfin, B., & Go, V. (1998). *A model for the development of Web-based, student-centered science education resources*. Paper presented at the Annual Meeting of the National Association for Research in Science Teaching (71st, San Diego, CA, April 19-22, 1998). 33pp. (ED 418 870). The purpose of this study was to evaluate The Student Genome Project, an experiment in Web-based genetics education. Over a two-year period, a team from New York University worked with a biology teacher and 33 high school students (N=33), and a middle school science teacher and a class of students (N=21) to develop a World Wide Web site intended to enable middle and secondary school students to learn the principles of molecular genetics in fun and engaging ways. A second major aspect of the project involved both the high school and middle school students working in pairs on genetics research projects by gathering survey data in their schools and data on the molecular genetics of their topic from the World Wide Web. Interactive Web pages and a Webboard were used to guide and mentor students during their research projects. Data sources included genetics literacy surveys, technology literacy surveys, postings on the Webboard, and interviews with teachers and students. Important factors involved in the design and implementation of the World Wide Web site were identified and used to develop a theoretical model of student-centered Web-based science education resources.

Quinlan, L. A. (1996). Customizing web documents for the classroom: An example from Lakeville High School's advanced composition class. *TechTrends, 41*(2), 27-30. (EJ 520 231). Discusses how to build customized World Wide Web documents; uses examples from an Advanced Composition class at Lakeville High School (Minnesota). Highlights four steps: (1) assessing student needs; (2) developing instructional goals and activities; (3) deciding on content; and (4) organizing and arranging the information into Web pages.

Tobiason, K. (1997). Tailoring the Internet to primary classrooms. *Technology Connection, 4*(2), 8-9. (EJ 543 127). Describes how to customize Internet resources for the elementary school classroom. Discusses bookmarking appropriate Web sites; arranging student-developed material for a Web page; creating a Hypertext Markup Language (HTML) unit Web page; posting Uniform Resource Locators (URLs) for sites supporting unit activities; and Internet training for teachers.

Conclusion

Conclusion

The Internet has been called the "Information Superhighway," with access points to and from different network locations and information sources. The Internet, as described in this text, is really less of an organized roadway, and more of a sea within a world of information and learning. Amid the murky waters, rocks, and even sharks, one can find the hidden treasures and can strengthen oneself in the journey.

As students embark on their travels to solve information problems, they can use the Big6 as their map. This set of questions can guide students through the world of information and direct them to the most appropriate path for a given question or task. Just as traveling by sea is not always the most effective or efficient means of transportation, the Internet is not always the best resource. (Readers will need to use their imaginations here, as the Internet often represents the quickest mode of accessing information while water transport represents the slowest method of travel.)

Information mentors can play many roles in this scenario. They can build the vessel on which students travel across the sea; they can provide the gentle wind guiding students away from the sea's dangers and toward more favorable routes; they can act as captains steering the way—and anything in between. Whatever role they choose, information mentors are responsible for helping students navigate the world of information effectively, efficiently, and safely.

Teachers, parents, online experts, Internet content providers, and others can help students understand how the Internet fits into the big picture and how to use it to meet specific goals and objectives. In carrying out the four roles suggested in this text—planning instruction, coaching students in their use of the Internet, communicating with students via the Internet, and designing effective educational content on the Web—information mentors can play an important part in students' learning.

In this information age, the only thing one can count on is change. The way information is packaged and presented and accessed today will be different tomorrow. Armed with the Big6 and well-planned instruction, students can successfully navigate the waters, airways, and highways of information now and in the future.

References

References

American Library Association/Association for Educational Communications and Technology. (1988). *Information power: Guidelines for school library media programs.* Chicago: Author. (ED 315 028)

American Library Association/Association for Educational Communications and Technology. (1998). *Information power: Building partnerships for learning.* Chicago and London: Author.

American Library Association Presidential Committee on Information Literacy. (1989). *Final report.* Chicago: Author. (ED 316 074)

Anglin, G. J. (Ed.). (1995). *Instructional technology: Past, present, and future.* (2nd ed.). Englewood, CO: Libraries Unlimited, Inc.

Bennet, D. T. (1997). Providing role models online. *Electronic Learning, 16*(5) (March/April 1997), p. 50-51. (EJ 559 726)

Bopp, R. E., & Smith, L. C. (1995). *Reference and information services: An introduction.* (2nd ed.). Englewood, CO: Libraries Unlimited.

Bruwelheide, J. H. (1995). *The copyright primer for librarians and educators.* (2nd ed.). Washington, DC: National Education Association and Chicago: American Library Association. (ED 384 363)

Buehler, M., & Jones, P. (1998). Netting the Big6: Integrating instruction, information, and the Internet. *The Big6 Newsletter, 2*(1), 1, 10-11, 13.

Clinton, W. J. (1997). State of the Union address: Call to action for American education in the 21st century. U.S. Department of Education. [Online]. Available: http://www.ed.gov/updates/PresEDPlan/part11.html (Accessed 23 May 2000).

Clinton, W. J. (1997). State of the Union address, February 4, 1997. [Online]. Available: http://www.whitehouse.gov/WH/SOU97/ (Accessed 23 May 2000).

Clinton, W. J. (1997). *Technological literacy,* (Part of President Clinton's call to action for American education in the 21st century) U.S. Department of Education. [Online]. Available: http://www.ed.gov/updates/PresEDPlan/part11.html (Feb. 1997).

Clyde, A. (1997). Information skills in an age of information technology. *Emergency Librarian, 24*(4), 48-50.

Cottingham, S. (1999). Internet 101: What is the Web? [Online]. Available: http://www2.famvid.com/i101/web.html (Accessed 23 May 2000).

Cottrell, J., & Eisenberg, M. B. (1997). Web design for information problem-solving: Maximizing value for users. *Computers in Libraries, 17*(5), 52-54, 56-57. (EJ 544 789)

Darrow, R. Big6 and the world wide web intro http://www.clovisusd.k12.ca.us/alta/ big6/default.htm (Accessed 8 June 2000).

Darrow, R. (1999). Use the Big6 to harness the Internet. *The Big6 Newsletter, 2*(3), 10-11, 13.

Dick, W., & Carey, L. (1996). The systematic design of instruction. (4th ed.). New York: HarperCollins.

Educational Resources Information Center. (1997). *Getting online: A friendly guide for teachers, students and parents.* [Brochure]. (ED 409 891)

Eisenberg, M. B. (1996). Take the Internet challenge: Using technology in context. In Full speed ahead on the Internet. *Book Report, 15*(2), 5-6.

Eisenberg, M. B., & Berkowitz, R. E. (1990). *Information problem-solving: The Big Six Skills approach to library and information skills.* Norwood, NJ: Ablex Publishing.

Eisenberg, M. B., & Berkowitz, R. E. (1996). *Helping with homework: A parent's guide to information problem solving.* Syracuse, NY: ERIC Clearinghouse on Information and Technology, Syracuse University.

Eisenberg, M. B., & Johnson, D. (1996). Computer skills for information problem-solving: Learning and teaching technology in context. *ERIC Digest.* Syracuse, NY: ERIC Clearinghouse on Information & Technology.

Eisenberg, M. B., Johnson, D., & Berkowitz, R. E. (1996). *Computer skills for information problem-solving: A curriculum based on the Big Six Skills approach.* In D. Johnson & M. B. Eisenberg, Computer literacy and information literacy: A natural combination. *Emergency Librarian, 23*(5), 12-16.

Eisenberg, M. B., & Berkowitz, R. E. (1998). The Big6 and student achievement: Report of an action research study. *The Big6 Newsletter, 2*(2), 1, 6-7, 15.

Eisenberg, M. B., & Berkowitz, R. E. (1999). The Big6 Skills™ curricula. [Online]. Available: http://www.big6.com/resources.htm#Big6Curricula (Accessed 8 June 2000).

Eisenberg, M. B., & Berkowitz, R. E. (1999). Promoting the Big6 (A Word from Mike and Bob), *The Big6 Newsletter, 2*(3), 2, 13.

Ekhaml, L. (1996). Making the most of e-mail: How to be concise, courteous, and correct online. *Technology Connection, 2*(10), 18-19.

Electronic Emissary. (1998). Electronic emissary home page. [Online]. Available: http://www.tapr.org/emissary/ (Accessed 23 May 2000).

El-Tigi, M., & Branch, R. M. (1997). Designing for interaction, learner control, and feedback during Web-based learning. *Educational Technology, 37*(3), 23-29.

Fayetteville-Manlius Schools. (1996). *Curriculum overview.* Grade 4. September 1996, (2nd ed.). Manlius, NY: Fayetteville-Manlius Schools.

Gagne, R. M., Briggs, L. J., & Wager, W. W. (1992). *Principals of instructional design.* (4th ed.). Fort Worth, TX: Harcourt Brace Jovanovich.

Gentry, C. G. (1995). Educational technology: A question of meaning. In G. J. Anglin (Ed.), *Instructional technology: Past, present, and future* (2nd ed., pp. 1-10). Englewood, CO: Libraries Unlimited, Inc.

Harasim, L., et al. (1995). *Learning networks.* Cambridge, MA: MIT Press.

Harris, J. (1998). *Virtual architecture: Designing and directing curriculum-based telecomputing.* Eugene, OR: International Society for Technology in Education.

Harris, J. and others. (1996). It's a simple idea, but it's not easy to do! Practical lessons in telementoring. *Learning and Leading with Technology, 24*(2), 53-57. (EJ 534 536).

International Society for Technology in Education. (1998). *National educational technology standards for students.* Eugene, OR: International Society for Technology in Education.

International Telementor Center. (1999). *HP telementor program overview.* [Online]. Available: http://www.telementor.org/hp/archive/itc.pdf (Accessed 23 May 2000).

Johnson, D., & Eisenberg, M. B. (1996). Computer literacy and information literacy: A natural combination. *Emergency Librarian, 23*(5), 12-16.

Jukes, I. (1997). Opening address to California School Library Association conference. Pasadena, CA. Thornburg Center for Professional Development.

Kasowitz, A. (1999). Digital reference services for K-12 education: AskA services. *ERIC Networker.* Syracuse, NY: ERIC Clearinghouse on Information & Technology.

Kosakowsi, J. (1998). The benefits of information technology. *ERIC Digest.* Syracuse, NY: ERIC Clearinghouse on Information and Technology. (ED 420 302)

Lankes, R. D. (1996). *The bread & butter of the Internet: A primer and presentation packet for educators.* Syracuse, NY: ERIC Clearinghouse on Information and Technology. (ED 402 924)

Lankes, R. D., & Kasowitz, A. S. (1998). *AskA starter kit: How to build and maintain digital reference services.* Syracuse, NY: ERIC Clearinghouse on Information and Technology. (ED 427 779)

Library, University of California, Berkeley. (1997). What is the Internet, the WWW, and Netscape? An Introduction. [Online]. Available: http://www.lib.berkeley.edu/TeachingLib/Guides/Internet/WhatIs.html (Accessed 23 May 2000).

Lindsay, L. (1996). *Web page design.* Peru, NE: Peru State College Library.

Little, T. (1998). The famous "banana split" lesson. *The Big6 Newsletter, 1*(4), 4-5.

Lowe, C. (1998). Reports from the front lines. *The Big6 Newsletter, 1*(4), 3, 15.

Mid-Continent Regional Educational Laboratory (McREL). (1996a). Language arts standards: Language arts (Langarts) 4.2.1. [Online]. Available: http://www.mcrel.org/standardsbenchmarks/benchmarks/langarts/4.2.1.html (Accessed 11 May 2000).

Mid-Continent Regional Educational Laboratory (McREL). (1997). "Geography standard 2, Grades 3-5, Benchmark 2" [Online]. Available: http://www.mcrel.org/standardsbenchmarks/benchmarks/geograph/2.2.2.html (Accessed 11 May 2000).

Miller, T. (1997). Tom Miller's presentation on "Interactive Demographics" at Editor & Publisher's Interactive Newspaper's '97 Conference in Houston, February 15, 1997. Emerging Technologies Research. [Online]. Available: http://etrg.findsvp.com/resfh/intnews.html (Accessed 6 May 1997).

National Council of Teachers of Mathematics. (1989). NCTM Standards: Table of contents. Curriculum and evaluation standards for school mathematics. Reston, VA: National Council of Teachers of Mathematics, 1989. [Online]. Available: http://www.enc.org/reform/journals/ENC2280/nf_280dtoc1.htm (Accessed 11 May 2000).

Online Safety Project. (1998). Kids' rules for online safety. [Online]. Available: http://www.safekids.com/kidsrules.htm (Accessed 11 May 2000).

Palgi, R. D. (1996). Rules of the road: Why you need an acceptable use policy. *School Library Journal*, 42(8), 32-33. (EJ 529 690)

Pappas, M. L. (1995). Information skills for electronic resources. *School Library Media Activities Monthly*, 11(8), 39-40.

Pappas, M. L. & Tepe, A. E. (1994). Information skills model. In *Teaching Electronic Information Skills*. McHenry, IL: Follett Software Company. pp. 1-7.

Paulu, N. (1995). Homework: A concern for the whole family ("Helping Your Child With Homework"). U.S. Department of Education: Office of Educational Research and Improvement. [Online]. Available: http://www.ed.gov/pubs/parents/Homework/pt2.html (Accessed 6 May 1997).

Provenzo, E.F. Jr. (1998). *Educator's brief guide to the Internet and the World Wide Web*. Larchmont, NY: Eye on Education.

Rakes, G. C. (1996). Using the Internet as a tool in a resource-based learning environment. *Educational Technology*, 36(5), 52-56.

Roblyer, M. D. (1998). The other half of knowledge. *Learning and Leading with Technology*, 25(6), 54-55.

Rowand, C. (1999). *Issue brief: Internet access in public schools and classrooms: 1994-1998*. Washington, DC: National Center for Education Statistics. (ED 428 755)

Schrock, K. (1996). Critical evaluation survey: Secondary school level. [Online]. Available: http://school.discovery.com/schrockguide/evalhigh.htm (Accessed 13 May 1997).

Schrock, K. (1998). Kathy Schrock's guide for educators—Critical evaluation surveys. [Online]. Available: http://discovery school.com/schrockguide/eval.html (Accessed 11 May 2000).

Schrock, K. (1999). The ABCs of web site evaluation: Teaching media literacy in the age of the Internet. *Classroom Connect's Connected Teacher*. [Online]. Available: http://www.connectedteacher.com/newsletter/abcs.asp (Accessed 8 June 2000).

Simpson, C. M. (1997). *Copyright for schools: A practical guide*. (2nd ed.). Worthington, OH: Linworth Publishing. (ED 406 987)

Small, R.V., & Arnone, M. P. (1998). WebMAC Senior, 3.1. Fayetteville, NY: Motivation Mining Company. Small, R. V., & Arnone, M. P. (1999a). Web site quality: Do students know it when they see it? *School Library Media Activities Monthly*, 15(6), 25-26, 30.

Small, R. V., & Arnone, M. P. (1999b). *WWW motivation mining: Finding treasure for teaching evaluation skills, Grades 7-12.* Worthington, OH: Linworth Publishing.

So… what about working with the very youngest? (1997). *The Big6 Newsletter, 1*(1), 16.

Spitzer, K. S., Eisenberg, M. B., & Lowe, C. A. (1998). *Information literacy: Essential skills for the information age.* Syracuse, NY: ERIC Clearinghouse on Information and Technology.

Sutton, S. (1999). StandardConnections™: "More like this". [Online]. Available: http://ericir.syr.edu/~ssutton/GEM/GEM_Standard_Connections.html (Accessed 11 May 2000).

The Math Forum. (1999). About the Math Forum. [Online]. Available: http://forum.swarthmore.edu/about.forum.html (Accessed 11 May 2000).

Tomei, L. A. (1996, September). Preparing an instructional lesson using resources off the Internet. *T.H.E. Journal, 24*(2), 93-95.

U.S. Congress (1994). Sec. 102. National education goals. http://www.ed.gov/legislation/GOALS2000/TheAct/sec102.html (Accessed 8 June 2000).

Wear, B. (1998). A handbook for HP mentors. [Online]. Available:http://www.telementor.org/hp/info/handbk1.html (Accessed 11 May 2000).

Weiss, J. (1996). The wiring of our children. *NewMedia, 6*(8), 36-37, 39.

Willard, N. (1996). K-12 acceptable use policies. [Online]. Available: http://www.erehwon.com/k12aup/index.html (Accessed 11 May 2000).

Yee, D. (1998). Telecommunications in middle years. The Global Schoolhouse. [Online]. Available: http://www.gsh.org/wce/archives/yee.html (Accessed 11 May 2000).

Appendices

Appendices

Appendix A: Getting Started on the Net—Courses and Resources

The following Web sites and ERIC resources are provided to help beginners become familiar with the Internet. Some resources are geared towards Internet users in general, while other resources are intended specifically for educators. This list of instructional and informational resources contains introductions, tips, definitions, and guidelines to help Internet novices become comfortable and efficient users of this valuable tool.

Internet Resources

Topic: General Audience

Beginner's Central
http://northernwebs.com/bc/
This 8-chapter online tutorial (complete with appendices) is designed specifically for newcomers to the Internet. There are links to each chapter (both the main chapter and contents of each).

The Beginner's Guide to Life on the Internet
http://www.screen.com/start/guide/
This online Web tutorial from Cochran Interactive includes basic information on general Internet concepts (e.g., search engines, netiquette) and applications (e-mail, FTP, etc.).

ICYouSee Guide to the World Wide Web
http://www.ithaca.edu/library/Training/ICYouSee.html
This self-guided Web training page is a project of the Ithaca College Library. It provides a user-friendly introduction to the Web that is organized around such questions as: "What can you do on the Web that is actually useful?," "What went wrong? or Why did it do that?" and "How can you create a Webpage for yourself?" The site includes a glossary of Web terminology and a guide to Internet search tools.

What is the Internet, the WWW, and Netscape? An Introduction
Teaching Library Internet Workshops, University of California, Berkeley
http://www.lib.berkeley.edu/TeachingLib/Guides/Internet/WhatIs.html
This Internet training site from the University of California, Berkeley, is a good introduction for people who are new to the Internet and World Wide Web. It includes the following links: What is the Internet?; What is the World Wide Web and What Makes it Work?; What is Netscape?; Getting Connected to the Internet; Links to a Glossary of WWW and Netscape Jargon; and a free drop-in Internet Courses Schedule, as well as LINKS to the rest of the UC Berkeley Teaching Library Internet Tutorial.

Topic: Education

WebTeacher
http://www.webteacher.org/winnet/indextc.html
This site, from the National Cable Television Association and TECH Corps., is a comprehensive, interactive, 80-hour, self-guided and self-paced tutorial, freely available to teachers over the Internet. Created by teachers, the service helps educators master the Internet and integrate new technologies into student learning. Teachers can learn to navigate the 'Net, link to educational Web sites, develop lesson plans, create their own home pages, find tips on Internet safety, and more.

School.Net Best Links
http://k12.school.net/links/
School.Net is a Web site that contains links to schools, educational information, and help with the Internet for teachers, students, and parents. Links on this page provide resources on connecting to the Internet, issues in education and educational products and services. Also see School.Net's Internet Glossary (*http://k12.school.net/help/glossary.network.cs2.html*) for definitions of technical Internet terms.

Web66: A K12 World Wide Web Project
http://web66.coled.umn.edu/
This site is designed to help introduce the Internet into K-12 schools and the curriculum. Available services include a registry of K-12 schools on the Web, resources and instructions for setting up Internet servers in schools, and information and resources for learning to find and use information on the Internet.

EdWeb HomeRoom
http://edweb.gsn.org/
This site provides a background on the roles and applications of the Web in education as well as guidelines for using Internet resources and tools. Features include an interactive crash course in HTML, links to educational resources on the Web, and discussion of issues in education reform for the 21st century and computers and K-12 students.

ICONnect: Online Courses—Learn to Use the Internet as a Curriculum Resource
http://www.ala.org/ICONN/onlineco.html
ICONnect, a technology initiative of the American Association of School Librarians (AASL), a division of the American Library Association (ALA), is designed to help students, library media specialists and teachers use the Internet in learning. Online courses include IBASICS—an introductory course for library media specialists—and advanced courses in topics such as navigating, searching, curriculum integration, telecollaboration, and developing a home page. Courses are conducted via e-mail.

ERIC Citations

Connecting K-12 schools to the information superhighway. Washington, DC: McKinsey & Co., Inc., 1995. (ED 393 397). This report discusses options for connecting K-12 public schools to the Internet. Applications and benefits of such connections are presented, as well as logistical and leadership challenges.

Jones, D. (1998). *Exploring the Internet using critical thinking skills: A self-paced workbook for learning to effectively use the Internet and evaluate online information*. New York, NY: Neal-Schuman Publishers, Inc. 94 pp. (ED 416 850). This workbook, intended for self-guided instruction or classroom use, teaches students how to navigate the Internet with a critical mind. It offers tips on Web searching, looking for reputable sources, identifying bias, manipulative reasoning, propaganda, irrelevant and misleading information, checking for accuracy and timeliness of information, learning Netiquette, and using online newsgroups. Also included are guidelines for citation styles for all types of Internet resources including Listserv messages, WWW, Gopher sites, FTP sites, and Usenet Groups. Thirteen chapters include: (1) "Course Goal and Objectives"; (2) "Map of the Workbook"; (3) "Caveats to the Learner"; (4) "Symbols Used in the Workbook"; (5) "Introducing Netscape"; (6) "Lesson One: Walking onto the Web"; (7) "Lesson Two: The Critical Thinker"; (8) "Lesson Three: Evaluating Sources"; (9) "Lesson Four: How Wide Is the Web?"; (10) "Lesson Five: All the News"; (11) "Lesson Six: Learning on the Web"; (12) "Lesson Seven: People Are Talking"; and (13) "Lesson Eight: Spinning Your Web." Includes graphs, index and glossary.

Simpson, C., & McElmeel, S. L. (1997). *Internet for schools* (2nd ed.). Worthington, OH: Linworth Publishing. 256pp. (ED 405 849). This book is designed as an introduction to the Internet and World Wide Web for teachers and school library media specialists. The book helps educators learn about the Internet and assists them in taking the lead in technology in their school. Librarians have a vested interest in learning about the Internet and its wealth of resources. As a worldwide network of electronic information, the Internet helps librarians provide resources that could not possibly be provided at the local level. As with any new information resource, librarians, teachers, and students need training and experience to become "power users." The book contains the following chapters: (1) What is the Internet? (2) Searching the Web; (3) Introducing the Internet to Students; (4) Introducing the Internet to Faculty and Staff; (5) Uses of the Internet in School Libraries; (6) Uses of the Internet in Specific Content Areas; (7) Getting Online; and (8) Internet Access Points. Appendices include an introduction to e-mail, file transfer protocol (FTP), World Wide Web (WWW), and transparency masters for providing training sessions. A glossary, URL (uniform resource locator) and e-mail address index, and subject index are provided.

Appendix B: Searching the Internet

A key component to Internet use is the searching process. Finding the sites you want out of the millions available can be tricky, if not frustrating. In order to save time and ensure a more productive search, the Internet user should be aware of all the searching tools available and the rules that accompany each one. The resources listed below offer information and instruction on getting the most out of Internet search tools.

AskScott Web Searching Tutorial
http://www.AskScott.com/
AskScott is a "virtual reference librarian" who helps people locate information on the Internet. The tutorial includes tips on how Web search engines work, how to select the proper search terms, how to combine search terms effectively, and a quiz on searching.

Finding Information on the Internet
http://www.lib.berkeley.edu/TeachingLin/Guides/Internet/FindInfo.html
This Internet workshop from The Teaching Library of the University of California, Berkeley, includes an introduction to the Internet, a glossary of terms, things to know before searching the World Wide Web, how to create search strategies, and how to refine your topic and identify the search tools to fit your needs. There are also well-designed pages on how to construct and refine searches for Infoseek, Hotbot, and AltaVista.

How to Use Boolean Logic
http://www.newsbank.com/whatsnew/boolean/
This page describes the general concepts of Boolean Logic through graphics and examples.

Internet Tips and Tricks for Searching the Net
http://www.tiac.net/users/hope/cil98/tips98.htm
Written by Hope N. Tillman and Walt Howe as a presentation for the Computers in Libraries '98 Conference, these suggestions offer obvious and not-so-obvious solutions to searching dilemmas.

The Search is Over: The Search-Engine Secrets of the Pros (by Adam Page)
http://www.zdnet.com/pccomp/features/fea1096/sub2.html
Published by PC Computing, this guide includes profiles of the top search engines as rated by experts. A table outlines the pros and cons of each search engine. A guide to Boolean logic is also included.

Sink or Swim: Internet Search Tools & Techniques By Ross Tyner, M.L.S., Okanagan University College
http://www.cln.org/~gateway/nuggets/96-97/0081.html
This site, designed as an instructional workshop, introduces the concept of Internet searching, describes and compares various search engines and subject guides, and offers search strategies and tips. Also provided are practice exercises, information on conducting people searches and a list of references regarding Internet searching.

Tutorial: Guide to Effective Searching of the Internet
http://thewebtools.com/searchgoodies/tutorial.htm
This site contains an excellent overview of how to conduct effective and successful Internet searches, covering 48 topics organized in 12 sections.

Web Searching Guide From the Internet Public Library
http://www.ipl.org/ref/websearching.html
This page offers links to and information regarding the IPL's "favorite" Internet search engines and catalogs.

Appendix C: Evaluation of Internet Sites

After a search process is completed, information mentors and students should evaluate individual Web sites. This is an important component of information problem-solving. The following sites and citations provide criteria for Web site evaluation that will help information mentors teach students to be critical thinkers and to design quality Internet resources for students.

Critical Thinking and Internet Resources
http://www.mcrel.org/resources/plus/critical.asp
This site, from Mid-Continent Regional Educational Laboratory (McREL), offers links to Web site evaluation criteria for educators, students and other Internet users, and presents content standards related to evaluating information resources.

Kathy Schrock's Guide for Educators—Critical Evaluation Surveys
http://discoveryschool.com/schrockguide/eval.html
This site offers critical surveys for elementary, middle, and secondary school students to use when evaluating Web sites. Also provided are links to other Web sites with evaluation criteria for educators and Web page designers.

National School Network Site Evaluation
http://nsn.bbn.com/webeval/form1.htm
This feedback form is designed for educators to provide comments regarding their satisfaction with Web sites on levels of educational value and design qualities. Instructions for review and listing of sites requesting reviews are included on linked pages.

Web Site Evaluation—A Collection of Research Papers and Surveys
http://web.syr.edu/~maeltigi/Research/RIGHT.HTM
The links on this page provide criteria that can be used to make judgments about educational Web sites in K-12 and higher education contexts.

ERIC Citations

Brandt, D. S. (1996). Evaluating information on the Internet. *Computers in Libraries, 16*(5), 44-46. (EJ 524 769). Evaluation of information found on the Internet requires the same assessment of reliability, credibility, perspective, purpose and author credentials as required with print materials. Things to check include whether the source is from a moderated or unmoderated list or FTP (file transfer protocol) site; directories for affiliation and biographical information; archives of author's work; and reviews of online lists.

Everhart, N. (1997). Web page evaluation: Views from the field. *Technology Connection, 4*(3), 24-26. (EJ 544 697). Presents a checklist for school librarians to use in evaluating World Wide Web pages. Highlights include content; authority; ease of navigation; the "experience"; use of graphics, sound, and video; treatment, including stereotyping and age appropriateness; speed and types of access; and costs and search engines.

Jones, D. (1998). *Exploring the Internet using critical thinking skills: A self-paced workbook for learning to effectively use the Internet and evaluate online information.* New York: Neal-Schuman Publishers, Inc. This workbook, intended for self-guided instruction or classroom use, teaches students how to navigate the Internet with a critical mind. It offers tips on Web searching, looking for reputable sources, identifying bias, manipulative reasoning, propaganda, irrelevant and misleading information, checking for accuracy and timeliness of information, learning Netiquette, and using online newsgroups. Also included are guidelines for citation styles for all types of Internet resources including Listserv messages, WWW, Gopher sites, FTP sites, and Usenet Groups. Thirteen chapters include: (1) "Course Goal and Objectives"; (2) "Map of the Workbook"; (3) "Caveats to the Learner"; (4) "Symbols Used in the Workbook"; (5) "Introducing Netscape"; (6) "Lesson One: Walking onto the Web"; (7) "Lesson Two: The Critical Thinker"; (8) "Lesson Three: Evaluating Sources"; (9) "Lesson Four: How Wide Is the Web?"; (10) "Lesson Five: All the News"; (11) "Lesson Six: Learning on the Web"; (12) "Lesson Seven: People Are Talking"; and (13) "Lesson Eight: Spinning Your Web." Includes graphs, index and glossary. (Contains 20 references.)

Rutkowski, K. (1996). Caught in the middle: U.S. middle schools on the Web. *MultiMedia Schools, 3*(5), 73-75. (EJ 534 469). The World Wide Web is one way for middle school students and teachers to demonstrate creativity and innovation. Effective Web sites from Eastchester Middle School (NY), Monroe Middle School (WY) and Olmsted Falls (OH) are highlighted. The VOICES (Vision, Originality, Integrity, Community, Empowerment, Structure) methodology for Web site evaluation is described.

Schrock, K. (1996). It must be true: I found it on the Internet! *Technology Connection, 3*(5), 12-14. (EJ 531 025). This article discusses the need for students to evaluate technical aspects and subject content of World Wide Web pages. Schrock includes a sample lesson plan and evaluation form for teaching critical evaluation of Web pages.

Schrock, K. (1998). Evaluation of World Wide Web sites: An annotated bibliography. *ERIC Digest.* ERIC Clearinghouse on Information & Technology. [Online]. Available: http://ericir.syr.edu/ithome/digests/edoir9802.html.

Symons, A. K. (1996). Intelligent life on the Web & how to find it. Http: The thinking librarian's Web guide. Part 1. *School Library Journal, 42*(3), 106-09. (EJ 521 774). Discusses the use of the World Wide Web in school libraries based on examples from Juneau-Douglas (Arkansas) High School. Highlights include using the Web for students' research, evaluating the quality of information found, criteria for selecting Internet resources, and creating a home page with Hypertext Markup Language.

Symons, A. K. (1997). Sizing up sites: How to judge what you find on the Web. The Smart Web Primer Part 2. *School Library Journal, 43*(4), 22-25. (EJ 543 163). Discusses how librarians can evaluate information obtained from the World Wide Web. Sources of reviews are described, explanations for 22 evaluation criteria, along with an example, are included, and the future of Web evaluation is considered.

Appendix D: Academic Standards on the Internet

Academic standards, either on the state, national or local level, provide a basis for curricula and learning goals. Educators, parents and educational content providers should be familiar with standards in order to provide services and guidance to help students achieve consistent goals. Since the passage of "Goals 2000: Educate America Act" in 1994, national attention has been focused on setting and maintaining standards, and a large amount of information has been made available to the public. The resources listed below provide access to goals and standards on national and state levels, and background knowledge on the creation of standards.

Achieve National Clearinghouse
http://www.achieve.org/
This clearinghouse offers a database of state academic standards in math, English, science, and history/social studies. Also included on the site are sample student works linked to the state standards, the clearinghouse's annual report, and links to other education organizations and Web sites.

Content Knowledge: A Compendium of Standards and Benchmarks for K-12 Education, McREL
http://www.mcrel.org/standards-benchmarks/
This site provides a database of national standards and benchmarks by subject and by grade level. Sources of standards include publications of national educational associations in different content areas. Subject-related Internet links are also included.

Developing Educational Standards
http://putwest.boces.org/Standards.html
This comprehensive site is a repository for information about educational standards and curriculum frameworks from all related Internet sources (national, state, local, and other).

Goals 2000: Educate America Act
http://www.ed.gov/legislation/GOALS2000/TheAct/index.html
This site contains the full text of the "Goals 2000: Education America Act"—a set of national education goals to be reached by the year 2000—presented by Congress in January 1994 and signed by President Clinton in March 1994.

Improving America's Schools: A Newsletter on Issues in School Reform
http://www.ed.gov/pubs/IASA/newsletters/standards/
This newsletter from the U.S. Department of Education explains the different types of standards and how they are established. One standard from the State of Delaware is provided as an example.

Sites Offering Academic and Skill Standards
http://www.ed.gov/G2K/standard.html
Provided by the United States Department of Education, this page contains links to sites describing academic and skills standards on national and state levels.

ERIC Citations

Goals 2000: Reforming Education To Improve Student Achievement. Report to Congress. (1998). Washington, DC: Office of Elementary and Secondary Education (ED). 56pp. (ED 420 918). The Goals 2000: Educate America Act, which became law in 1994 and was amended in 1996, emphasizes student learning through a long-term, broad-based effort to promote coherent and coordinated improvements in education. A report of this act's influence on education is presented here. The text provides a history of Goals 2000, including the legislation, amendments, and state planning that went into the act. It outlines the strategic role of Goals 2000, focusing on state-level support for reform, sustaining the reform effort, and supplementing ongoing reform. How the act emphasizes standards-based reform and presents content and performance standards are described, along with accountability for improvement, assessment, student performance, accountability, teacher preparation, community and parental involvement, and coordinated change. How the Goals were formulated to serve all children and how they are being maintained are discussed, as are coordination efforts, professional development and preservice education, assessment details, the use of data and research, and sustaining the momentum. Three appendices offer information on funding allocation, the Education Flexibility Demonstration Program, and parent information and resource centers. It is claimed that 47 states plus the District of Columbia and Puerto Rico now have comprehensive Goals 2000 plans for education reform and that all states are developing systems that hold districts and schools accountable for student performance. "Goals 2000 Funding Allocation," "Education Flexibility Demonstration Program (Ed-Flex)," and "Parent Information and Resource Centers" are appended.

Goals 2000 and World-Class Standards on the Internet. *ERIC/AE Digest*. ERIC Clearinghouse on Assessment and Evaluation, Washington, DC (ED 385 610). [Online]. Available: http://www.ed.gov/databases/ERIC_Digests/ed385610.html (11 May, 2000). The digest highlights Internet resources related to Goals 2000 and World Class standards. Topics include legislation and policy, parent assistance, local and state assistance, national and international programs and pointers to "Goals 2000" on the Internet. See the ERIC Clearinghouse on Assessment and Evaluation (ERIC/AE) gopher site (gopher.cua.edu, special resources, ERIC, Goals 2000) for information on accessing resources mentioned.

Appendix E: Locating and Designing School Web Pages

The following sites contain links to school home pages both in and outside of the United States and provide tips for creating school Web pages.

Internet Resources

HotList of K-12 Internet School Sites
http://www.gsn.org/hotlist/index.html
This site contains links to U.S.-based schools, districts, state departments of education, and state home pages. It is part of the Global Schoolhouse site from the Global SchoolNet Foundation and is a member of The Classroom Connection.

TENET Web: Schools on the Web
http://www.tenet.edu/education/main.html
This site from Texas Education Network (TENET) contains links to World Wide Web sites at K-12 schools in Texas and around the world, U.S. colleges and universities, online course materials and Web site development resources.

Web 66: International WWW School Registry
http://web66.umn.edu/schools.html
This registry provides links to K-12 schools and districts on the Internet. Schools are encouraged to register their home pages with Web 66. A link to information on setting up Web servers is included.

Yahoo! Links to K-12 Schools
http://dir.yahoo.com/Education/K_12/Schools/
This directory includes links to schools on the WWW from all over the world. Schools are organized by type (i.e. Montessori, Gifted Youth, Boarding Schools, etc.) and level.

ERIC Citations

Barkhouse, N. (1997). Grasping the thread: Web page development in the elementary classroom. *Emergency Librarian, 24*(3), 24-25. (EJ 538 040). Describes how a Canadian teacher and her second and third graders developed a Web page using minimal technology. Discusses individual and collaborative writing projects, simple and cheap Web file storage, HTML coding, hardware, hypertext links, multimedia projects, Internet connections, funding, student goals, motivation, audience response, and listservs for teachers wanting to start Web work or find partners for joint projects.

Buchanan, M. (1997). So you want to write a school home page but don't know where to begin. *Technology Connection, 4*(4), 26-27. (EJ 550 879). Discusses aspects of school home pages: school policy, parental involvement and concerns, Internet access and commercial providers, HTML programming, links to other Web pages, graphics, and the importance of proofreading.

Hewitt, W. J. (1998). *8 Easy ways to develop your Web page.* 10pp. (ED 420 298). This paper presents ideas to help educators develop a Web page geared to supplement classroom instruction. These suggestions include: (1) keep it simple, initially; (2) organize; (3) use tables; (4) apply color; (5) provide images; (6) consult others; (7) get class feedback; (8) consider a discussion forum; and (9) link to other sites that relate to the class material.

Lindsay, L. (1996). *Web page design.* Peru, NE: Peru State College Library. 9pp (ED 399 971). Designing a Web home page involves many decisions that affect how the page will look, the kind of technology required to use the page, the links the page will provide, and kinds of patrons who can use the page. The theme of information literacy needs to be built into every Web page; users need to be taught the skills of sorting and applying information to their individual needs. Web page design should involve: (1) planning ahead and writing a style sheet to define the who, what, and how of the pages; (2) keeping the pages simple; (3) designing the pages for fast use and allowing the user to have a choice between text and graphics; (4) making the pages readable; (5) showing the interdisciplinary and hierarchical nature of information and knowledge; and (6) keeping the links up-to-date. While HTML programming does not define the document structure as desktop publishing, the time is quickly coming when the principles of desktop publishing will be used in Web publishing. The Web designer who wants to design a Web page that all browsers can use will use the HTML2 standard. There are resources designed to help with a home page and to evaluate information on the Internet for use when designing Web pages. Two such resources are highlighted, as well as a sample of the Peru State College Library (Nebraska) home page.

Vandegrift, K. E. (1996). Build a Web site with a brain. Http: The thinking librarian's Web guide, Part 2. *School Library Journal, 42*(4), 26-29. (EJ 523 162). Describes procedures for librarians interested in building a World Wide Web site. Highlights include hypertext markup language; home pages; determining audiences and purposes; promoting safety; the planning process, including text length and density, links to external sites, and maintenance; and copyright concerns.

Appendix F: Citing Internet Sources

Information mentors should encourage students to cite information from all sources, whether print or electronic. The following links and ERIC citations provide guidelines for citing Web sites, e-mail messages and other Internet-based resources based on standard style formats.

Internet Resources

Bibliographic Formats for Citing Electronic Information
http://www.uvm.edu/~ncrane/estyles/
This site provides guidelines for citing resources on the World Wide Web based on the citation formats of APA and MLA. These formats are based on Li and Crane's *Electronic Styles: A Handbook for Citing Electronic Information* (1996), by Information Today, Inc.

The Columbia Guide to Online Style
http://www.columbia.edu/cu/cup/cgos/idx_basic.html
This site offers guidelines for citing electronic sources in both a humanities style and a scientific style.

Documenting Sources from the World Wide Web
http://www.mla.org/style/sources.htm
These guidelines on citing WWW sources are authorized by the Modern Language Association (MLA). Includes a list of information that should be contained in a works-cited page and several examples.

Meriam Library: Citation Formats
http://www.csuchico.edu/lref/newciting.html
This California State University site contains links to guidelines for citing Internet and print sources. Linked sites offer guidelines that are adapted mostly from MLA and APA formats.

Nueva Library Research Goal
http://www.nueva.pvt.k12.ca.us/~debbie/library/research/research.html
This site is designed to help K-12 students develop research and information literacy skills. Guidance is offered on citing electronic and print sources using the MLA format. The site also includes examples and practice opportunities for citing resources as well as tips on conducting research.

ERIC Citations

Carroll, R. (1997). Documentation of electronic sources. *Business Education Forum, 51*(4), 7-10. (EJ 542 220). Presents alternative methods for citing electronic sources found on the Internet, giving examples that describe type of medium and availability as well as standard bibliographic information.

Turell, L. (1997). *Library online! A guide to computer research.* Parsippany, NJ: Good Apple. 99pp. (ED 400 830). The world of electronic technology is opening up vast new opportunities for learning, gathering, and sharing information. This guide is for teachers and students in grades 4-8 to learn how to use electronic tools to conduct research to find information at school or around the world. The guide includes introductory pages for each topic, student activity pages, and sample information pages, such as a printout of books on the topic of cooking, printouts of book citations, and listings of Internet addresses. Topics covered include: (1) "The Basics of the Computer"; (2) "The Electronic Card Catalog"; (3) "Computerized Search Strategies"; (4) "CD-ROM Research Databases"; (5) "Reading Computer Printouts"; (6) "Citing Electronic Resources"; and (7) "Online: The Internet."

Appendix G: Online Safety

Many parents and educators are concerned that students will access resources on the Internet that are inappropriate. The Internet sites and ERIC citations listed below can help prepare parents, educators and students for safe use of the Internet, without restricting students from exploring and learning. Suggestions include forming acceptable use policies, blocking and filtering software, and educating parents and the community about the educational benefits of the Internet.

Internet Resources

Censorship in the Information Age
http://www.nueva.pvt.k12.ca.us/~debbie/library/policies/censor96.html
This article, written by Debbie Abilock, librarian from a K-8 school in California, originally appeared in *California Education*, April/May 1996: 22-31. Guidelines are provided for educators and librarians considering Internet use in the schools.

The Internet Advocate: A Web-based Resource Guide for Librarians and Educators Interested in Providing Youth Access to the Net
http://www.monroe.lib.in.us/~lchampel/netadv.html
This guide informs librarians and educators of issues to be aware of when offering Internet access to children. Topics include responding to inaccurate perceptions of porn on the net, promoting positive examples of youth Internet use, developing an "Acceptable Use Policy" (AUP), and understanding software to block Internet sites and related safety/censorship issues. This site also includes contact information for organizations committed to electronic freedom of information.

Internet Parental Control Frequently Asked Questions (FAQ)
http://www.vtw.org/pubs/ipcfaq
The Voters Telecommunications Watch (VTW) provides this guide to assist parents, legislators, educators, and the public in making decisions regarding acceptable use of the Internet. Existing solutions are discussed such as parental control, government restrictions and various systems. Most of the original product research for parental control tools was done by the Center for Democracy and Technology.

Keeping Kids Safe! An Internet Hotlist on "Keeping Kids Safe in the World of Technology"
http://www.kn.pacbell.com/wired/fil/pages/listkeepingki.html
This site includes resources on libraries and the Internet, online safety guides, and filtering and blocking software. Also includes a list of search engines for kids.

K-12 Acceptable Use Policies
http://www.erehwon.com/k12aup/index.html
This site offers resources for educators who are developing Internet policies. Templates for various policy documents are included, as well as a document outlining educational and legal issues involving K-12 acceptable use policies. Information on the site is provided by Nancy Willard, Information Technology Consultant, Eugene, Oregon.

Safe Kids Home Page
http://www.safekids.com/
This site includes a link to "Child Safety on the Information Highway" by Lawrence J. Magdid and the Center for Missing and Exploited Children. It also includes guidelines for parents, kids' rules for online safety, and other information on how to keep children safe online.

ERIC Citations

Futoran, G. C. and others. (1995). The Internet as a K-12 educational resource: Emerging issues of information access and freedom. *Computers & Education, 24*(3), 229-36. (EJ 508 648). Explores issues of K-12 educators incorporating wide-area networking into the curriculum and becoming consumers and providers of materials on the Internet; factors include decision making, legal problems, and student behaviors. Describes a K-12 project called Common Knowledge: Pittsburgh.

Keeping your child safe online. How to protect your children from the dangers of cyberspace. (1997). *Our Children, 23*(3), 32-33. (EJ 557 645). Three major ways parents can restrict the material their children experience online include using commercial online services with parental control features, installing other parental control software, and using the Platform for Internet Content Selection. Parents must protect their children's privacy, be aware of commercialism online, and take action if incidents occur online.

Lazarus, W., & Lipper, L. (1996). *The parents' guide to the information superhighway: Rules and tools for families online*. Santa Monica, CA: Parent's Guide. Computers and online services are becoming a part of children's lives. This guide is designed to introduce parents to the Information Superhighway and to parenting in a world of computers and new forms of media. Prepared by the Children's Partnership, with assistance from the National PTA and the National Urban League, this guide provides tools and rules for parents to use with children at home, at school, and in the community. The guide helps parents gain an understanding of the technology, learn what is at stake for them and their children, and how they can help their children reap the benefits of the information age. The following sections are included: (1) "What is the Information Superhighway?"; (2) "What's at Stake— Why Computers Matter to Your Child"; (3) "What Does Using Computers Actually Do for Your Child?"; (4) "When Is Your Child Ready?"; (5) "Have We Been Here Before?"; (6) "Some Basic Rules"; (7) "Setting Up To Go Online"; (8) "Alternatives to a Home Computer"; (9) "How Can You Find Good Places To Go and Things To Do Online?"; (10) "How Can You Keep Your Child Safe Online?"; (11) "At School—Getting Involved with Technology"; and (12) "Helping Ensure that All Children Have an On-Ramp." Includes appendices with resources for further help and a glossary.

Magid, L. J. (1996). Protecting your child on the information highway: What parents need to know. *Montessori-Life* (8)1, 26. (EJ 520 499). Discusses how parents can reduce the risks of inappropriate Internet use and ensure positive online experiences for their children. Gives guidelines for family rules and personal rules that each young user should know and understand.

Palgi, R. D. (1996). Rules of the road: Why you need an acceptable use policy. *School Library Journal*, 42(8), 32-33. (EJ 529 690). With increasing Internet access, library media specialists are implementing acceptable use policies to govern student conduct online. Policy components include definition and purpose; rights, responsibilities, and risks; penalties; and parental consent. Effective policies have input from all community members, are concise, and serve as guidelines to meet educational goals. Provides a list of model policies on the Internet.

Sanchez, R. (1996). Students on the Internet: Can you ensure appropriate access? *School Administrator*, 53(4), 18-22. (EJ 522 755). Congress recently approved a Communications Decency Act (part of the sweeping Telecommunications Act of 1996) that criminalizes the act of making pornography available to minors on the Internet. School districts can avoid the darker corners of online access and reassure parents by adopting acceptable use policies, board of education policies, or filters. A sidebar lists World Wide Web resources. (Available on the Internet at http://www.aasa.org/SA/april01.htm)

Simpson, C. (1996). Right filter for the wrong addresses: Regulating net access. *Book Report*, 15(2), 17-18. (EJ 529 707). Guides librarians in evaluating "filtering" software that schools may purchase for restricting access to potentially inappropriate Internet sites. This article discusses the workings of filtering programs and practical and ethical questions such as: how sites are restricted, who decides, and whether transactions are monitored. Purchasers should also know if documentation, updates, and installation are included in the cost.

Truett, C. and others. (1997). Responsible Internet use. *Learning and Leading with Technology,* 24(6), 52-55. (EJ 543 188). Provides advice for making school Internet-use guidelines. Outlines responsible proactive use of the Internet for educators and librarians, discusses strengths and weaknesses of Internet blocking software and rating systems, and describes acceptable-use policies (AUP). Lists resources for creating your own AUP, Internet filtering software, and Internet rating systems.

Appendix H: Designing Web Sites

The resources below provide introductory information on creating Web sites using Hypertext Markup Language (HTML). Educators, students and others can refer to these resources in designing sites for instruction as well as projects and classroom presentations. Alternatives to HTML are also addressed in some resources.

A Beginner's Guide to HTML
http://www.ncsa.uiuc.edu/General/Internet/WWW/HTMLPrimer.html
The guide is an introduction to HTML. Links to additional Web-based resources about HTML and other related aspects of preparing files are also provided.

CNET: The Computer Network
http://builder.com/Authoring/Basics/
This article (which is part of CNET's Builder.com) includes a very basic walkthrough on using HTML for creating a web page. This tutorial covers a variety of topics, from including graphics and links to backgrounds and creating lists. It also contains a handy HTML quick reference section and links to additional resources, like articles on Web design and HTML editors.

Delivering Instruction on the World Wide Web
http://www.csuhayward.edu/ics/htmls/Inst.html
This document for educators presents basic issues involved in Web-based instruction, it's design, and its delivery. This section "Creating your pages" focuses on the technical issues of Web page design: basics of HTML, multimedia, clickable maps, forms, advanced HTML, and new technologies.

Writing HTML: A Tutorial For Creating Web Pages
http://www.mcli.dist.maricopa.edu/tut
Writing HTML was created to help teachers create learning resources that access information on the Internet, but is accessible to anyone who wants to learn how to use HTML. This tutorial prepares readers to construct a series of linked Web pages for any subject that includes formatted text, pictures, and hypertext links to other Web pages on the Internet.

How to Order ERIC Documents

Individual copies of ERIC documents are available in either electronic full-text, microfiche, or paper copy from the ERIC Document Reproduction Service (EDRS), 7420 Fullerton Road, Suite 110, Springfield, VA 22153-2852; some are available only in microfiche. Information needed for ordering includes the ED number, the number of pages, the number of copies wanted, the unit price, and the total unit cost. Sales tax should be included on orders from Maryland, Virginia, and Washington, DC.

Please order by ED number, indicate the format desired (electronic full-text, microfiche, or paper copy), and include payment for the price listed plus shipping. Call EDRS at 1-800-443-ERIC (or 703-440-1400) or e-mail EDRS customer service department: service@edrs.com, for information on pricing, shipping costs and/or other services offered by the contractor. For more information, see *http://www.edrs.com*

Inquiries about ERIC may be addressed to the ERIC Clearinghouse on Information & Technology, 621 Skytop Road, Suite 160, Syracuse University, Syracuse, NY 13244-5290 (800-464-9107), e-mail: eric@ericir.syr.edu; or ACCESS ERIC, 2277 Research Boulevard, 7A, Rockville, MD 20850 (800-LET-ERIC), e-mail: *acceric@accesseric.org* or URL *http://www.accesseric.org*

Journal Articles
Copies of journal articles can be found in library periodical collections; through interlibrary loan; from the journal publisher; or from article reprint services such as the UMI/InfoStore (1-800-248-0360), UnCover Company (1-800-787-7979), or Institute for Scientific Information (ISI) (1-800-336-4474). Information needed for ordering includes the author, title of article, name of journal, volume, issue number, page numbers, date, and EJ number for each article. Fax services are available.

What is ERIC?
ERIC, the Educational Resources Information Center, is a national education information system sponsored by the Office of Educational Research and Improvement in the U.S. Department of Education. The main product of ERIC is a bibliographic database containing citations and abstracts for more than 1 million documents and journal articles published since 1966. Most of the document literature cited in ERIC can be read in full text at any of the 900+ libraries or institutions worldwide holding the ERIC microfiche collection. In addition, users can purchase copies of ERIC documents from the ERIC Document Reproduction Service. Journal articles cited in ERIC can be obtained at a subscribing library, through interlibrary loan, or from an article reprint service

How do I find information in ERIC?
The ERIC Database can be searched online or in print indexes. Over 3,000 libraries and information centers subscribe to one or both of these monthly indexes. The database can also be searched online: (a) through a computer-based information retrieval service; (b) by CD-ROM; (c) on a locally mounted system, which may be accessible through the Internet; or (d) Internet: *http://ericir.syr.edu/Eric/*.

What is ERIC/IT?
The ERIC Clearinghouse on Information & Technology, or ERIC/IT, is one of 16 clearinghouses in the ERIC system. It specializes in library and information science and educational technology. ERIC/IT acquires, selects, catalogs, indexes, and abstracts documents and journal articles in these subject areas for input into the ERIC database.

Among the topics covered in library and information science are:
- Management, operation, and use of libraries and information centers
- Library technology and automation
- Library education
- Information policy
- Information literacy
- Information storage, processing and retrieval
- Networking

Topics covered in educational technology include:
- Design, development, and evaluation of instruction
- Computer-assisted instruction
- Multimedia
- Telecommunications
- Distance education

What is available from ERIC/IT?

Each year, ERIC/IT publishes Monographs, and Digests in the fields of educational technology and library and information science. Our semiannual newsletter, *ERIC/IT Update*, announces new clearinghouse products and developments, and *ERIC/IT Networkers* provide helpful information for using ERIC-related resources on the Internet.

Publications
- Digests provide brief overviews of topics of current interest and references for further reading
- Monographs feature trends and issues analyses, synthesis papers and annotated bibliographies
- *ERIC/IT Update* is a semiannual newsletter

User Services
- Response to inquiries about ERIC and matters within the ERIC/IT scope area
- Workshops and presentations about ERIC and database searching
- Assistance in searching the ERIC database

AskERIC
- Internet-based question answering service for educators
- AskERIC Virtual Library, an Internet site of education-related information resources including lesson plans, InfoGuides, listservs and much more
  E-mail: askeric@askeric.org
  Internet: http://www.askeric.org

Would you like to submit your work to ERIC?

Have you written materials related to educational technology or library and information science that you would like to share with others? ERIC/IT would be interested in reviewing your work for possible inclusion in the ERIC database. We actively solicit documents from researchers, practitioners, associations, and agencies at national, state, and local levels. ERIC documents include the following and more:

- Research Reports
- Program Descriptions
- Instructional Materials
- Conference Papers
- Teaching Guides
- Opinion Papers

How do I find out more?
For additional information about ERIC or about submitting documents, or for a current publications list, contact:

ERIC Clearinghouse on Information & Technology
621 Skytop Road, Suite 160
Syracuse University
Syracuse, New York 13244-5290
R. David Lankes, Director
Telephone: (315) 443-3640   Fax: (315) 443-5448   (800) 464-9107
E-mail: eric@ericir.syr.edu   *http://ericir.syr.edu/ithome*

Questions about the ERIC system can also be directed to:
ACCESS ERIC
2277 Research Boulevard, 6L
Rockville, Maryland 20850
Telephone: (800) LET-ERIC
E-mail: accesseric@accesseric.org
       http://www.accesseric.org

ERIC Clearinghouses
- Adult, Career, and Vocational Education
- Assessment and Evaluation
- Community Colleges
- Counseling and Student Services
- Disabilities and Gifted Education
- Educational Management
- Elementary and Early Childhood Education
- Higher Education
- Information & Technology
- Languages and Linguistics
- Reading, English, and Communication
- Rural Education and Small Schools
- Science, Mathematics, and Environmental Education
- Social Studies/Social Science Education
- Teaching and Teacher Education
- Urban Education

Support Components
- ERIC Document Reproduction Service
  Telephone: (800) 443-ERIC (3742)
- ERIC Processing and Reference Facility
  Telephone: (800) 799-ERIC (3742)

Index

Index

I

information literacy, 2, 3, 5, 7, 10, 11, 14, 15, 16, 19, 46, 53, 76, 109, 126, 132, 134, 135, 136, 147, 148, 154
information literate, 5
information mentor, 2, 3, 4, 5, 7, 10, 11, 14, 15, 16, 19, 46, 53, 76, 82, 86, 87, 109, 110, 121, 126, 130, 142, 148
Information Power: Building Partnerships for Learning, 10, 132
information problem-solving, 14, 15, 16, 46, 77
information problem-solving model, 2, 5, 12, 13, 86, 108, 109, 123
information problem-solving process, 2, 4, 5, 7, 12, 14, 16, 18, 22, 27, 35, 40, 46, 53, 54, 63, 86, 89, 95, 99, 118, 115
information problem-solving skill, 2, 5, 11, 15, 34, 39, 89, 108, 109
information searching skills, 7
Information Seeking Strategies, 5, 6, 7, 9, 15, 16, 28, 31, 32, 46, 60, 64, 67, 69, 73, 77, 78, 91, 96, 97, 98, 99, 113, 114, 117, 119, 122
Information Skills Model, 7, 11, 135
information use monitoring, 54, 55
instructional design, 10-13, 20, 34, 44, 108-111, 123, 133
instructional goals, 22, 101, 110, 127
instructional need, 21, 34, 40
instructional objectives, 19, 20
instructional resources, 109, 123
integrated curriculum, 19
integrated lessons, 20
International Telementor Center, 25, 85, 88, 102, 134
Internet educational potential, 19
Households using the, 54
methods for incorporating into instruction, 26
use for instruction, 19
Internet Challenge, 11, 133
Internet coaching, 53, 63, 76, 130
Internet Content Developers, 2, 110
Internet Proficiency, 58
Internet Safety, 19, 101, 139

K

KidsConnect, 84, 104, 106

L

lesson plans, 23, 27, 45, 47, 112, 115, 139, 154
sample, 115
library media specialist, 2, 10, 11, 16, 19, 20, 23, 28, 29, 33, 46, 52, 53, 57, 60, 63, 64, 69, 70, 75, 91, 104, 113, 114, 119, 121, 125, 140, 151
Location & Access, 5, 6, 9, 15, 22, 23, 24, 27, 28, 31, 32, 53, 54, 55, 60, 64, 91, 97, 98, 99, 113, 114, 119, 122
LOCATION AND ACCESS, 26, 46, 77, 78, 96, 97

M

MAD Scientist Network, 84
models for teaching information literacy, 5
motivational features, 110
motivational quality, 110

N

National Education Goals Year 2000, 54
National Educational Technology Standards (NETS) Project, 8
Netiquette, 24, 79, 138, 140, 143

O

objectives, 10, 12, 13, 14, 18, 19, 20, 22, 24, 25, 27, 28, 30, 31, 32, 34, 35, 36, 39, 40, 42, 43, 44, 53, 88, 113, 114, 115, 121, 130, 140, 143, 149
Online Safety, 26, 57, 75, 79, 135, 149, 150

P

parents, 2, 3, 4, 10, 11, 12, 19, 20, 21, 46, 52-59, 75-80, 84, 87, 90, 112, 130, 133, 135, 139, 144, 149, 150, 151,
permission, 37, 42, 55, 58, 88
Privacy, 77, 80, 88, 101, 150

Q

Quality criteria, 88

R

resource quality, 19, 57

S

Safety, 12, 19, 26, 52, 55, 57, 79, 88, 90, 101, 135, 139, 147, 149, 150
school library media specialist, 7, 10, 11, 46, 91, 97, 99, 114, 124, 140
student and classroom management, 19
Subject Area Telementors, 86, 101
synchronously, 83
Synthesis, 5, 6, 9, 15, 16, 22, 26-30, 32, 39, 41, 46, 54, 56, 61, 67, 72, 73, 75, 77, 78, 94, 97, 100, 113, 115, 118, 120, 122,
systematic approach to planning instruction, 20, 44
systematic approach to problem solving, 5, 54
systems approach model, 20

T

target objectives, 22, 35
Task Definition, 5, 6, 9, 15, 16, 31, 32, 46, 59, 63, 67, 68, 73, 77, 78, 90, 96-99, 111, 113, 114, 117, 119, 122
"Technology Foundation Standards," 8
technological literacy, 3, 132
telecollaboration, 83, 140
telecommunication activities, 86
telementoring, 13, 25, 37, 42, 82-90, 93, 94, 97, 100-103, 105, 109, 134
activities. See* facilitators, 86, 101
Women in Science, Engineering, and Computing, 85
teleresearch, 83

U

Use of information, 5, 6, 9, 10, 11, 15, 16, 22, 23, 27, 28, 30, 46, 53, 54, 55, 61, 66, 67, 71, 73, 75, 77, 78, 82, 93, 96, 97, 99, 113, 114, 118, 119, 122

W

Web evaluation criteria, 58, 110
Web site evaluation instruments, 116
Website development, 115